THIRD EDITION

Vocabulary
for
GCSE
SPANISH

Revised for the New
GCSE specifications

Geoff Taylor

Reprinted in 2003
Nelson Thornes Ltd
Delta Place
27 Bath Road
CHELTENHAM
GL53 7TH
United Kingdom

03 04 05 06 07 / 10 9 8 7 6 5 4 3

A catalogue record for this book is available from the British Library

ISBN 0 7487 6292 2

Page make-up by TechSet

Printed in Croatia by Zrinski

Contents

Introduction

◆ **Aims**

The aim of this book is to provide you with the vocabulary you need in the early years of learning Spanish. You will find it particularly useful in Years 10 and 11 to help prepare you for the GCSE Spanish examination. It is based on the specifications of the main examination boards and includes most of the words you will need for **Foundation** and/or **Higher Tier**. Obviously the lists are not prescriptive and you can expect to come across one or two unfamiliar words in the examination as well.

◆ **How the book is arranged**

Words are set out in easy to understand topic areas. They are also grouped in short blocks that go together in some way so that you will find them easier to learn. **Some words are printed in blue. These are basic words that you really must learn thoroughly.** However, if you are hoping to attain a really good grade then obviously you will need to extend your vocabulary and learn many of the other words as well. Many of the words are presented in phrases at the end of each topic, which you should find useful in your speaking and writing exams or when writing a letter. There are also activities and puzzles spread throughout the book to give further practice. At the back of the book there is a useful section on Building up Vocabulary, Words to Watch Out For, and Writing Tips. There are also some blank pages at the very end of the book where you can add any further words or phrases that you find useful.

◆ **How do I learn vocabulary?**

1   The learning of vocabulary (like the learning of grammar) is absolutely essential if you are going to make any real progress in Spanish.
2   Try to set yourself realistic targets – say you will learn so many new words every week, or day.
3   Get someone else (a member of your family or a friend) to test you.
4   Make learning cards to help you remember those words that are causing problems.
5   If you have a computer, you could devise a simple program to reinforce the vocabulary.

There is no doubt that as your vocabulary increases, so too will your confidence. You will become increasingly better equipped to tackle work in all skill areas of the language, whether in class, for homework or in exams. Of course, if you have a good working vocabulary, any visit you make to a Spanish-speaking country will be that much more enjoyable.

Yourself and Others

◆ **Foundation words**

Name:

llamarse	to be called
mi, mis	my
el nombre (de pila)	first name
el apellido	surname
se escribe	it is spelled
presentar	to introduce
la identidad	identity
el carnet de identidad	identity card
señor	Mr, Sir
señora	Mrs, Madam
señorita	Miss

Age:

la edad	age
tener… años	to be… years old
cumplir	to reach the age of

el cumpleaños	birthday
el santo	Saint's day
nacer	to be born
nací	I was born
el nacimiento	birth
la fecha de nacimiento	date of birth
✓ el lugar de nacimiento	place of birth

Nationality:

la nacionalidad	nationality
ser (soy)	to be (I am)
inglés, inglesa	English
escocés, escocesa	Scottish
galés, galesa	Welsh
irlandés, irlandesa	Irish
británico	British

◆ **Foundation phrases**

Me voy a presentar.	I'm going to introduce myself.
Me llamo Karen y tengo quince años.	My name is Karen and I'm 15 years old.
¿Cómo se escribe?	How do you spell it?
Soy escocesa.	I'm Scottish.
Nací en Edimburgo.	I was born in Edinburgh.
Tengo 14 años.	I'm 14 years old.
¿Cuántos años tienes?	How old are you?

Copy out and fill in your details:

Nombre _____

Apellido _____

Fecha de nacimiento _____

Lugar de nacimiento _____

Nacionalidad _____

◆ **Higher words**

el apodo   nickname

◆ **Higher phrases**

Nací en mil novecientos ochenta y seis.   I was born in 1986.
Soy Géminis.   I'm a Gemini.

	Acuario		Tauro		Leo		Escorpión
	Piscis		Géminis		Virgo		Sagitario
	Aries		Cáncer		Libra		Capricornio

A P P E A R A N C E

◆ **Foundation words**

Build:

ser (soy)	to be (I am)	los ojos	eyes
soy	I am	azules	blue
bastante	quite	grises	grey
muy	very	marrones/oscuros	brown
ni... ni...	neither... nor...	negros	black
alto	tall	verdes	green
bajo	small		
delgado	thin	**Hair:**	
gordo	fat	el pelo	hair
grueso	stout, heavily built	corto	short
		largo	long
Looks:		liso	straight
guapo	good looking, beautiful	rizado	curly
		castaño	brown
feo	ugly	rubio	blond
moreno	dark skinned/haired	pelirrojo	ginger
pálido	pale	calvo	bald
		el bigote	moustache
		la barba	beard
Eyes:			
tener (tengo)	to have (I have)		

◆ **Foundation phrases**

Tengo el pelo negro y corto y los ojos verdes.   I've got short, black hair and green eyes.
Soy bastante delgado.   I'm quite thin.

Face:

la cara	face
redonda	round
cuadrada	square

Other features:

llevar	to wear
las gafas	glasses

las lentillas, los lentes de contacto	contact lenses
la peca	freckle
medir (mido)	to measure (I measure)
pesar	to weigh
parecerse a (me parezco a)	to look like (I look like)

◆ **Foundation phrases**

Me parezco a mi padre.	I look like my dad.
¿A quién te pareces?	What do you look like?
Peso cincuenta y siete kilos.	I weigh 57 kilos.
Mido un metro setenta y cinco centímetros.	I measure 1 metre 75.

◆ **Higher words**

el flequillo	fringe
la cola de caballo, la coleta	pony tail

CHARACTER AND PERSONAL RELATIONSHIPS

◆ **Foundation words**

el carácter	character	cortés	polite
la calidad	quality	creativo	creative
la personalidad	personality	cruel	cruel
		débil	weak
agradable	nice	aficionado al deporte/ deportivo	sporty
agresivo	aggressive		
alegre	happy	desobediente	disobedient
amable	kind	dinámico	dynamic
amistoso	friendly	egoísta	selfish
animado	lively	elegante	smart
antipático	nasty, unpleasant	emprendedor	pushy
atento	thoughtful	estúpido	stupid
atrevido	daring	extrovertido	extrovert
callado	quiet	famoso	famous
capaz	capable	formal	well-behaved
cariñoso	affectionate	fuerte	strong
célebre	famous	generoso	generous
celoso	jealous	goloso	greedy
cobarde	cowardly	gracioso	funny
comprensivo	thoughtful	hablador, habladora	chatty, talkative
contento	happy, content	honrado	honest

impaciente	impatient	serio	serious
inocente	innocent	severo	strict
insolente	insolent, cheeky	simpático	nice
inteligente	intelligent	sincero	sincere
listo	clever	tímido	shy
mal educado	rude, ill-mannered	tonto	daft, silly
		torpe	clumsy
mentiroso	untruthful	trabajador, trabajadora	hard-working
mezquino	mean, stingy		
nervioso	nervous	travieso	naughty
obediente	obedient	triste	sad
optimista	optimistic	valiente	brave
orgulloso	proud		
paciente	patient	el comportamiento	behaviour
perezoso	lazy	comportarse	to behave
pesimista	pessimistic	llevarse bien con	to get on well with
pobre	poor		
popular	popular	llevarse mal con	to get on badly with
práctico	practical		
prudente	wise	el sentido del humor	sense of humour
responsable	responsible	estar de buen humor	to be in a good mood
rico	rich		
seguro de sí mismo	self confident	estar de mal humor	to be in a bad mood
sensible	sensitive		

◆ Foundation phrases

Soy bastante perezosa y habladora. — I'm quite lazy and chatty.
Mi hermano es muy travieso. — My brother is very naughty.
Me llevo bien con mis padres. — I get on well with my parents.

◆ Higher words

afable	pleasant, nice	distraído	absent minded
afortunado	lucky	insoportable	unbearable
aplicado	studious	pesado	dull, boring
artístico	artistic	sordo	deaf
bondadoso, bueno	kind	terco, testarudo	stubborn
ciego	blind	tranquilo	calm, placid
cojo	crippled, lame	tutear	to address someone as "tu"
compasivo	compassionate		

◆ Higher phrases

Me da cien patadas. — He is a pain in the backside.
Es una persona divertidísima. — She is great fun.
Nos llevamos estupendamente. — We get on really well.
La conozco desde hace dos años. — I've known her for two years.

9

FAMILY AND FRIENDS

◆ Foundation words

la familia	family	el nieto	grandson
los padres	parents	la nieta	grand-daughter
la madre	mother	el primo, la prima	cousin
el padre	father	el sobrino	nephew
(la) mamá	mum	la sobrina	niece
(el) papá	dad	el tío	uncle
la madrastra	**stepmother**	la tía	aunt
el padrastro	**stepfather**		
el hermano	brother	el amigo, la amiga	friend
la hermana	sister	el compañero,	friend,
mayor	elder	la compañera	companion
menor	younger	mejor	best
el hermanastro	**stepbrother**	el novio	fiancé
la hermanastra	**stepsister**	la novia	fiancée
el gemelo, el mellizo	**twin**	la boda	wedding
el hijo	son	**el casamiento**	**marriage**
la hija	daughter	casarse con	to marry
los hijos	children	casado	married
único	only	**el matrimonio**	**married couple**
el bebé	baby	soltero	single
el niño	little boy	divorciado	divorced
la niña	little girl	**divorciarse**	**to divorce**
el muchacho, chico	boy	**el divorcio**	**divorce**
la muchacha, chica	girl	**separado**	**separated**
el chico	boy (teenage)	el viudo	widower
la chica	girl (teenage)	la viuda	widow
el esposo, el marido	husband		
la esposa, la mujer	wife	el amor	love
la pareja	**couple**	el abrazo	embrace
los parientes	**relatives**	abrazar	to embrace
el abuelo	grandfather	el beso	kiss
la abuela	grandmother	**besar**	**to kiss**

◆ Foundation phrases

¿Cuántas personas hay en tu familia?	How many people are in your family?
Hay cuatro personas.	There are four people.
Soy hijo único.	I'm an only child.
Mi amigo/amiga se llama…	My friend is called…
Es muy simpático/a.	He/she is very nice.

10

◆ Higher words

el crío	kid, child	el noviazgo	engagement
el cuñado	brother-in-law	la niñez	childhood
la cuñada	sister-in-law	conocerse	to get to know someone
el suegro	father-in-law		
la suegra	mother-in-law	cohabitar	to live together
el yerno	son-in-law	echar de menos	to miss (someone)
la nuera	daughter-in-law		
el bautismo	christening	enamorado	in love
la primera comunión	first communion	enamorarse (de)	to fall in love (with)

◆ Higher phrases

Estoy enamorado de una chica fenomenal.	I'm in love with a fantastic girl.
Somos novios.	We are engaged.
No quiero casarme hasta que tenga treinta años.	I don't want to get married till I'm thirty.

PETS

el animal (de compañía)	animal, (pet)	el periquito	budgie
el caballo	horse	el pez	fish
la cobaya	guinea pig	el pez dorado, el pez de colores	goldfish
el conejo	rabbit		
el gato	cat	la rata	rat
el perro	dog	el ratón	mouse
el pájaro	bird	la tortuga	tortoise

◆ Foundation phrases

¿Tienes un animal de compañía?	Have you got a pet?
Tengo un perro negro.	I've got a black dog.
Se llama Snoopy.	It's called Snoopy.
Es bastante grande.	It's quite big.
No me gustan los gatos.	I don't like cats.

◆ Higher words

el cachorro	puppy	la serpiente	snake
el gatito	kitten	feroz	ferocious
la jaula	cage	ladrar	to bark
el loro	parrot	morder	to bite

11

◆ Higher phrases

Tenía un pez pero murió hace un año.	I had a fish but it died a year ago.
Me gustaría tener un ratón pero a mi madre no le gustan.	I'd like to have a mouse but my mother doesn't like them.
Tenemos un perrito que es muy mono.	We have a puppy who is very cute.

PROHIBIDO PERROS SUELTOS

PERROS

- **RESIDENCIA** canina. Reserva El Rincón. Infórmese, visítenos. 2166557, 8620657.
- **RESIDENCIA** – adiestramiento. 8410950.
- **GARDEN-CAN.** Residencia canina. 8156596.
- **HOTEL** Barajas. 7477366.
- **COLLIES** (Lassie). 2304990, 8130142.
- **ADIESTRAMIENTOS** Verdú. Profesionalidad. 4640377.
- **LABRADORES,** cachorros. 8110652.
- **YORKSHIRE** superselección. 2744038, 6581362.
- **COCKER,** teckel campeones. 744038, 6581362.
- **PASTORES** alemanes, doberman, cachorros adiestrados. 2744038, 6581362.
- **BICHON** frise. 2744038, 6581362.

Pérdidas

PERDIDA en zona Almagro-Castellana perra mestiza de alzada media, pelo corto y color negro y canela. Atiende por «Laila». Lleva collar de cadena con tira de cuero verde. Se recompensará devolución. ☎ 4193520.

What does this lost dog look like?

ANIMALES

Gatitos persas, *pedigree,* campeones. ☎ 239 54 14.

Home Life

WHERE YOU LIVE

◆ **Foundation words**

Location:

vivir	to live
en	in
el norte	north
el este	east
el sur	south
el oeste	west
el noreste, nordeste	north-east
el noroeste	north-west
el sudeste, sureste	south-east
el suroeste	south-west
Londres	London
la aldea	village
el campo	country
la ciudad	city
la costa	coast
la montaña	mountain
el pueblo	town
a orillas del mar	at the seaside
las afueras	outskirts
la capital	capital
el centro	centre
el barrio	district
la región	region
la zona	area
agradable	pleasant
céntrico	central
concurrido	busy
industrial	industrial
precioso	lovely
residencial	residential
ruidoso	noisy
sucio	dirty
tranquilo	quiet
turístico	touristy
la dirección	address
el domicilio	home address (on a form)

el código postal	post code
la avenida	avenue
la calle	street
la carretera	main road
estar situado	to be situated
estar a… kilómetros (de)	to be… kilometres (from)
estar a … metros (de)	to be… metres (from)
estar cerca de	to be near to
estar lejos de	to be far from

Type of accommodation:

el apartamento	apartment
el bloque	block (of flats)
la casa	house
la casa adosada	semi-detached house
el chalé/chalet	semi-detached house, villa
la finca	country house
la granja	farm
el piso	flat
alquilado	rented
amueblado	furnished
antiguo	old
cómodo	comfortable
con aire acondicionado	with air conditioning
con calefacción central	with central heating
moderno	modern
nuevo	new
particular	private
el dueño	owner
el vecino	neighbour

◆ Foundation phrases

¿Dónde vives?	Where do you live?
Vivo en un pequeño pueblo en la costa.	I live in a small town on the coast.
Vivo en el noreste de Inglaterra.	I live in the north-east of England.
El barrio donde vivo es sucio.	The area I live in is dirty.
No hay mucho que hacer.	There is not a lot to do.

◆ Higher words

la casa de campo	country house	la zona verde	green belt
la casa adosada	semi-detached house	cercado por, rodeado de	surrounded by
el chalet independiente	detached house	campestre	country (adj)
el edificio de pisos	block of flats	lujoso, de lujo	luxury
el rascacielos	skyscraper	municipal	municipal, town (adj)
la urbanización	housing development	pintoresco	picturesque
de ladrillo	made of brick	privado	private
de madera	made of wood	solitario	lonely, remote
de piedra	made of stone	la callejuela	lane
colocar	to position, place	el camino	small road
situado	situated	el ciudadano	town dweller, citizen
los alrededores	surroundings		
el pueblecito	small town	el inquilino	tenant
la vecindad	neighbourhood	amoblar/amueblar	to furnish
la zona urbanizada	built-up area	mudarse de casa	to move house

◆ Higher phrases

Vivo en el sexto piso en un edificio de pisos.	I live on the sixth floor in a block of flats.
Mi tío tiene una casa de campo lujosa.	My uncle has a luxurious country house.

ROOMS AND PARTS OF THE HOUSE

◆ Foundation words

el cuarto	room	la escalera	stairs
abajo	downstairs	el garaje	garage
arriba	upstairs	el jardín	garden
la planta baja	ground floor	el pasillo	landing
el primer piso	the first floor	el patio	patio
el balcón	balcony	el sótano	basement
la cocina	kitchen	el tejado	roof
el comedor	dining room	el techo	ceiling
el salón	living room	el suelo	floor
el cuarto de baño	bathroom	la puerta	door
el desván	loft	la ventana	window
el dormitorio	bedroom		

◆ Foundation phrases

¿Cuántos cuartos hay en tu casa?	How many rooms are there in your house?
¿Puedes describir tu dormitorio?	Can you describe your bedroom?
Tengo mi propio dormitorio.	I have my own bedroom.
Comparto mi dormitorio con mi hermano menor.	I share my bedroom with my younger brother.

◆ Higher words

el cuarto para invitados	spare room	el trastero	junk room

FURNITURE AND CONTENTS

◆ Foundation words

los muebles	furniture	la chimenea	fireplace
la cocina de gas	gas cooker	las cortinas	curtains
la cocina eléctrica	electric cooker	el cuadro	picture
el congelador	freezer	la librería	bookcase
el fregadero	sink	la mesa	table
el frigorífico	fridge	la moqueta	fitted carpet
la lavadora	washing machine	la papelera	waste-paper basket
el lavavajillas	dishwasher		
la nevera	fridge	el reloj	clock
		la silla	chair
la alfombra	rug, carpet	el sillón	arm-chair
el aparador	sideboard	el sofá	sofa, settee
la butaca	armchair	el televisor	TV set

15

el vídeo	video recorder	el escritorio	desk
		el estante	shelf
el aseo	toilet	la estantería	shelves
el baño	bath	la lámpara	lamp
el cuarto de baño	bathroom	el lector de compact disc	CD player
la ducha	shower		
el espejo	mirror	la manta	blanket
el lavabo	wash basin	la pared	wall
el retrete	toilet	el póster	poster
		el tocador	dressing table
el armario	wardrobe, cupboard		
la cama	bed	el árbol	tree
la cómoda	chest of drawers	la flor	flower
el despertador	alarm clock	la planta	plant
el equipo de música	hi-fi system	el césped	lawn

◆ **Foundation phrases**

En mi dormitorio hay una cama, un armario y una lámpara.	In my bedroom there is a bed, a wardrobe and a lamp.
Las paredes son azules y las cortinas son grises.	The walls are blue and the curtains are grey.
Tengo pósters de Newcastle United.	I have posters of Newcastle United.

◆ **Higher words**

los azulejos	tiles	la persiana	blinds, shutters (inside)
la bañera	bath		
el grifo	tap		
el horno	oven	la almohada	pillow
el microondas	microwave oven	el cojín	cushion
el enchufe	power point	la colcha	bedspread
la secadora	tumble dryer	el colchón	mattress
la baldosa	floor tile	el edredón	eiderdown, duvet
el parqué/parquet	parquet flooring	la sábana	sheet
el rellano	landing		
la cerradura	lock	el papel pintado	wallpaper
cerrar con llave	to lock	la cafetera	coffee pot
la contraventana	shutters (outside)	el cenicero	ash tray
		la tetera	teapot

DAILY ROUTINE

◆ **Foundation words**

acostarse (me acuesto)	to go to bed (I go to bed)	arreglarse	to get ready
		cepillar	to brush
afeitarse	to shave	dormir (duermo)	to sleep (I sleep)

dormirse	to go to sleep	el almuerzo	lunch
(me duermo)	(I go to sleep)	merendar	to have a
ducharse	to have a shower		snack/tea
lavarse	to get washed	la merienda	snack/tea
levantarse	to get up	cenar	to have supper
limpiarse los dientes	to clean teeth	la cena	supper
peinarse	to comb hair	comer	to eat
ponerse la ropa	to put on clothes	la comida	the meal
(me pongo)	(I put on)		
quitarse la ropa	to take off clothes	el cepillo	brush
tumbarse	to lie down	el cepillo de dientes	tooth brush
vestirse (me visto)	to get dressed	la pasta de dientes	tooth paste
	(I get dressed)	el champú	shampoo
		el jabón	soap
desayunar	to have breakfast	la toalla	towel
el desayuno	breakfast	el papel higiénico	toilet paper
almorzar (almuerzo)	to have lunch	el secador de pelo	hair dryer
	(I have lunch)		

◆ **Foundation phrases**

¿A qué hora te levantas normalmente?	What time do you normally get up?
Me levanto a las ocho menos cuarto.	I get up at quarter to eight.
¿Qué haces después?	What do you do next?
Me lavo y me peino.	I get washed and comb my hair.
¿A qué hora te acuestas?	What time do you go to bed?
Suelo acostarme a las diez y media.	I usually go to bed at half past ten.
¿Puedo ducharme?	Can I have a shower?
Normalmente desayuno a las ocho.	I usually have breakfast at eight o'clock.

◆ **Higher words**

la siesta	nap	el maquillaje	make-up
echar una siesta	to take a nap	quedarse en la cama	to have a lie in
maquillarse	to put on make-up		(in bed)

◆ **Higher phrases**

Después de levantarme me ducho y entonces me visto enseguida.	After getting up I have a shower and then I get dressed straightaway.
Suelo echar una siesta por la tarde.	I usually have a nap in the afternoon.
Normalmente me quedo en la cama el domingo por la mañana.	I normally have a lie in on a Sunday morning.

JOBS AROUND THE HOUSE

◆ Foundation words

los quehaceres	household jobs	lavar el coche	to wash the car
las tareas	chores	lavar la ropa	to wash the clothes
ayudar	to help		
arreglar	to tidy	limpiar	to clean
cocinar	to cook	pasar la aspiradora	to vacuum
cortar el césped	to cut the grass	planchar	to iron
fregar (friego) los platos	to do (I do) the washing up	poner (pongo) la mesa	to set (I set) the table
hacer (hago) la cama	to make (I make) the bed	preparar la comida	to prepare the food
hacer la compra	to do the shopping	quitar la mesa	to clear the table
ir (voy) de compras	to go (I go) shopping	trabajar en el jardín	to work in the garden

◆ Foundation phrases

¿Ayudas a tus padres en casa?	Do you help your parents in the house?
Generalmente lavo los platos y hago la cama.	I usually do the washing up and make my bed.
Los fines de semana hago la compra con mi padre.	At weekends I do the shopping with my dad.
A veces paso la aspiradora.	I sometimes do the vacuuming.

◆ Higher words

la tarea	task, job	llevar al perro de paseo	to take the dog for a walk
de la casa	household	el cortacésped	lawnmower
barrer	to sweep	la plancha	iron
la limpieza	cleaning	el trapo (del polvo)	duster
dar de comer al perro	to feed the dog	regar	to water

◆ Higher phrases

¿Puedo ayudarte a fregar los platos?	Can I help you to wash the dishes?
Mi padre no hace nada para ayudar en casa.	My dad does nothing to help in the house.
Pon la mesa y siéntate a comer.	Set the table and sit down to eat.
Cuido a los niños cuando mis padres salen.	I look after the children when my parents go out.
En el verano corto el césped.	I cut the grass in summer.

School

◆ **Foundation words**

el bolígrafo (boli)	biro	la mesa	table
el borrador	blackboard duster	el monitor	monitor
		el ordenador	computer
la calculadora	calculator	la página	page
la carpeta	file, folder	el papel	paper
la cartera	school bag	la pizarra	blackboard
el cassette (casete)	cassette player	la puerta	door
el cuaderno	exercise book	la regla	ruler
el diccionario	dictionary	el rotulador	felt-tipped pen
el estuche	pencil case	la silla	chair
la goma (de borrar)	rubber	el sacapuntas	pencil sharpener
el lápiz	pencil		
los lápices de colores	coloured pencils	el teclado	key-pad
		el texto	text
el libro	text book	las tijeras	scissors
el mapa	map	la ventana	window

◆ **Higher words**

los auriculares	headphones	el micrófono	microphone
la barra de cola, pegamento	glue stick	el pegamento	glue
		la perforadora	hole punch
el cartucho	cartridge	el proyector	projector
el certificado	certificate	el sujetapapeles	paper clip
la cinta adhesiva, el celo	sellotape	la tinta	ink
la grabadora	tape recorder	la tiza	chalk

WORKING IN THE CLASSROOM

◆ **Foundation words**

pasar lista	to call the register	apagar	to switch off (the light)
ausente	absent		
presente	present	buscar	to look for, get
levántate	stand up (1 pupil)	callarse	to keep quiet
levantaos	stand up (class)	cerrar	to close
siéntate	sit down (1 pupil)	contestar	to answer
sentaos	sit down (class)	copiar	to copy
abrir	to open	corregir	to correct

19

describir	to describe	sacar	to take out
la descripción	description	subrayar	to underline
dibujar	to draw	tener razón	to be right
diseñar	to sketch	no tener razón	to be wrong
encender	to switch on (light)	tocarle a uno	to be one's turn
entender (entiendo)	to understand	(el turno)	
	(I understand)	te toca a ti	it's your turn
escribir	to write	trabajar	to work
escuchar	to listen		
hablar	to talk	el acento	accent
hacer	to make, do	la frase	sentence
hacer preguntas	to ask questions	la letra	letter
la encuesta	survey	la palabra	word
la entrevista	interview	en borrador	in rough
levantar la mano	to put up your hand	en limpio	in neat
		las reglas	rules
leer	to read	masculino	masculine
mirar	to look	femenino	feminine
pedir	to ask for	correcto	correct
pedir prestado	to borrow	falso	false
poner (pongo)	to put (I put)	verdad	true
preguntar	to ask	mentira	false
preparar	to prepare	querer decir	to mean
prestar	to lend	significar	to mean
pronunciar	to pronounce		

◆ **Foundation phrases**

¡Sacad los cuadernos!	Take out your exercise books!
No entiendo.	I don't understand.
¡Repite por favour!	Repeat please!
¿Cómo se dice… en español?	How do you say… in Spanish?
¿Qué es… en inglés?	What is… in English?
¿Qué significa?	What does it mean?
¿Qué quiere decir?	What does it mean?
¿Cómo se pronuncia?	How is it pronounced?

◆ **Higher words**

asistir	to attend	hacer novillos	to truant
borrar	to rub out, erase	inscribir	to enrol
discutir	to discuss, argue	tocar el timbre	to ring the bell
enseñar	to teach	las cifras	numbers
equivocarse	to make a mistake	castigado	in detention
hacer experimentos	to do experiments	el esfuerzo	effort

20

◆ Higher phrases

María no asistió a la clase.	María did not attend the class.
Me gusta mucho hacer experimentos en las clases de química.	I love doing experiments in chemistry lessons.
No se puede fumar en el colegio.	You can't smoke at school.

PLACES IN SCHOOL

◆ Foundation words

la escuela	primary school	la clase	classroom
el colegio (el cole)	secondary school (up to 14)	el despacho	office
		el gimnasio	gym(nasium)
el instituto	secondary school (14–18)	las instalaciones	facilities
		el laboratorio	laboratory
mixto	mixed	el pasillo	corridor
el aula (f)	classroom	el patio	yard
la biblioteca	library	la sala de actos	hall
la cancha de tenis	tennis court	la sala de profesores	staff room
el comedor	dining room	el taller	workshop
el campo de deportes	playing field		

◆ Higher words

el internado	boarding school	el vestuario	changing room

SUBJECTS AND OPINIONS

◆ Foundation words

la asignatura	subject	la geografía	geography
el arte dramático	drama	la historia	history
el alemán	German	la informática	IT
la biología	biology	el inglés	English
las ciencias	science	la lengua	language
la cocina	cookery, food technology	la literatura	literature
		las matemáticas	maths
el comercio	business studies	la música	music
el dibujo	art	la orientación profesional	(vocational) guidance
la educación física	PE		
el español	Spanish	la química	chemistry
la ética	ethics	la religión	RE
la física	physics	la tecnología	technology
el francés	French	los trabajos manuales	CDT

21

SCHOOL

aburrido	boring	interesante	interesting
aburrirse	to be (get) bored	interesarse (en)	to be interested (in)
difícil	difficult	obligatorio	obligatory
duro	hard	opinar	to think of
estupendo	great	práctico	practical
fácil	easy	útil	useful

◆ Foundation phrases

¿Cuántas asignaturas estudias?	How many subjects do you study?
Estudio siete: matemáticas, inglés…	I study seven: maths, English…
Me gusta el español.	I like Spanish.
No me gusta nada la geografía.	I don't like geography at all.
Me gustan las ciencias.	I like science.
No me gustan las matemáticas.	I don't like maths.
Me encantan los idiomas.	I love languages.
Creo que las ciencias son muy útiles.	I think that science is very useful.
¿Cuál es tu asignatura favorita?	What is your favourite subject?
Prefiero el español porque es interesante.	I prefer Spanish because it is interesting.

◆ Higher words

abandonar una asignatura	to drop a subject	se me da bien…	I'm good at…
la formación sexual	sex education	se me da mal…	I'm bad at…

◆ Higher phrases

¿Cuánto tiempo hace que aprendes el español?	How long have you been learning Spanish?
Hace tres años que lo aprendo.	I've been learning it for three years.
En mi opinión las clases son demasiado largas.	In my opinion lessons are too long.
Se me da muy bien la historia.	I'm very good at history.
Se me da mal la física.	I'm weak in physics.
La encuentro difícil y pesada.	I find it hard and boring.

THE SCHOOL DAY

◆ Foundation words

las clases	classes, lessons	volver (vuelvo)	to return
el horario	timetable		(I return)
comenzar (comienzo),	to start (I start)	el recreo	break
empezar (empiezo)		la hora de comer	dinner time
durar	to last	después	after
terminar	to finish	después de las clases	after school
ir (voy) al colegio	to go (I go) to	el trimestre	term
	school	tener (tengo) que	to have (I have) to
la lección	lesson	llevar	to wear
llegar	to arrive	el uniforme	uniform
regresar	to return	la insignia	badge

◆ Foundation phrases

Las clases empiezan a las nueve y diez y terminan a las tres y veinticinco.	Classes start at 9.10 a.m. and finish at 3.25 p.m.
Hay cinco clases al día.	There are five lessons a day.
Las lecciones duran una hora.	Lessons last one hour.
Durante el recreo juego al fútbol o charlo con mis amigos.	During break I play football or chat to my friends.
Tengo que llevar uniforme.	I have to wear a uniform.
Hago mis deberes a las siete.	I do my homework at seven o'clock.

PEOPLE IN SCHOOL

◆ Foundation words

el alumno, la alumna	pupil	estricto	strict
el director	headmaster	respetar	to respect
la directora	headmistress	el respeto	respect
el estudiante	student	desobedecer	to disobey
el profesor/la	teacher	castigar	to punish
profesora		el castigo	punishment

◆ Foundation phrases

En mi colegio hay mil alumnos.	In my school there are a thousand pupils.
Mi profesor de español es simpático.	My Spanish teacher is nice.

◆ Higher words

el conserje	caretaker	el maestro	primary school teacher
el interno	boarder		

EXAMS AND TESTS

◆ Foundation words

aprobar (apruebo)	to pass (I pass)	sacar malas notas	to get bad marks
el bachillerato	school leaving exam	la presentación (oral)	(oral) presentation
los deberes	homework	el proyecto	project
el examen	exam	la prueba	test
la nota	mark	repasar	to revise
sacar buenas notas	to get good marks	suspender	to fail
		tener éxito	to be successful

◆ Foundation phrases

No me gustan los exámenes. — I don't like exams.
Siempre saco buenas notas en español. — I always get good marks in Spanish.
En mi presentación oral voy a hablar de… — For my oral presentation I'm going to talk about…

◆ Higher words

el bachillerato superior	higher certificate (= A level)	la EGB (Educación General Básica)	(Age 6–14)
el control	test	la FP (Formación Profesional)	(Age 14+)
copiar	to copy, cheat	el BUP (Bachillerato Unificado y Polivalente)	(Age 14–17)
el diploma	diploma	el COU (Curso de Orientación Universitaria)	(Age 17+)
la evaluación	assessment		
el examen de prueba	mock exam		
hacer trampa	to cheat		

◆ Higher phrases

No vale la pena hacer trampa. — It's not worth cheating.
El año que viene estudiaré para el bachillerato superior. — Next year I will study for A level.

EXAM LANGUAGE

completa… la tabla	complete… the table
contesta… las preguntas	answer… the questions
da… tus razones	give… your reasons
…tu opinión	…your opinion
decide… si es verdad, mentira o no se sabe	decide… if it is true, false or you don't know
escoge… la frase correcta	choose… the correct sentence
escribe… la letra	write… the letter
…el número	…the number

escucha… la conversación	listen to… the conversation
…la entrevista	…the interview
estudia… la información, las noticias	study… the information
explica… la diferencia	explain… the difference
haz… una lista	make… a list
haz corresponder… las frases	match up… the sentences
incluye… los detalles siguientes	include… the following information
indica… los errores	point out… the mistakes
…con una equis (✗)	mark… with an ✗
…con una marca (✓)	mark… with a ✓
justifica… tu opinión	justify… your opinion
lee… el artículo	read… the article
…la carta	…the letter
…el folleto	…the brochure
pon… en orden	put… in order
…una equis (✗) en la casilla correcta	…an ✗ in the correct box
…una marca (✓) en la casilla correcta	… a ✓ in the correct box
rellena… los detalles en español	fill in… the details in Spanish
…los espacios	…the gaps
…el formulario	…**the form**
…la ficha	…the registration form

You may also need:

añade	add	encuentra	find
busca	look for	imagina	imagine
cambia	change	menciona	mention
compara	compare	mira	look at
decide	decide	prepara	prepare
describe	describe	subraya	underline
empareja	match up	sugiere	suggest

◆ **Ejercicio**

Unjumble the letters to make eight school subjects.
Try to do this exercise without looking back.

1. SENIACIC ....

2. JOBUDI ....

3. GILENS ....

4. ICCANO ....

5. THARIOSI ....

6. MANLEA ....

7. SAMICU ....

8. GORENILI ....

(Answer on page 109)

The World of Work

FUTURE PLANS

◆ **Foundation words**

en el futuro	in the future
la ambición	ambition
esperar	to hope
querer (quiero)	to want (I want)
me gustaría, quisiera	I would like
voy a	I'm going to
pensar (pienso)	to intend (I intend)
continuar	to continue
terminar	to finish
los estudios	studies
la calificación	qualification
calificado	qualified, skilled
capacitar	to train someone for
el certificado	certificate
la formación profesional	vocational training
dejar el colegio	to leave school
ir a la universidad	to go to university
buscar	to look for, get
encontrar, hallar	to find
comenzar, empezar	to start
la carrera profesional	career
el empleo	job
el puesto	post, position
el trabajo	work
emplear	to employ

el empleado	employee
pagar	to pay
pagar bien	to pay well
pagar mal	to pay badly
la paga	pay
el sueldo	salary
ganar	to earn
ganarse la vida	to earn one's living
hacerse	to become
ser	to be
trabajar (en)	to work (in)
la compañía	company
la empresa	firm
la fábrica	factory
el hospital	hospital
la industria	industry
la oficina	office
la tienda	shop
en el extranjero	abroad
trabajar con	to work with
los animales	animals
los ordenadores	computers
la gente	people
los niños	children
el aprendiz	apprentice
el aprendizaje	apprenticeship
tener éxito	to be successful
tener suerte	to be lucky
la entrevista	interview

◆ **Foundation phrases**

¿Qué vas a hacer el año que viene?	What are you going to do next year?
El año que viene quiero buscar empleo.	Next year I want to look for a job.
Espero seguir estudiando en el instituto.	I hope to carry on studying at school.
Pienso estudiar ciencias.	I intend to study science.
Si apruebo mis exámenes quisiera ir a la universidad.	If I pass my exams I'd like to go to university.
Quiero tener éxito en el futuro.	I want to be successful in the future.
Voy a trabajar en una oficina.	I'm going to work in an office.

26

◆ **Higher words**

aconsejar	to advise	asalariado	salaried, paid
me apetece	I fancy	bancario	bank (adj),
no me apetece	I don't fancy		banking
ampliar la experiencia	to broaden	al aire libre	in the open air
	one's	el ejército	army
	experience	la marina	navy
la responsabilidad	responsibility	los negocios	business
la ventaja	advantage	estresante	stressful
la desventaja	disadvantage	exigente	demanding
la dificultad	difficulty	a tiempo parcial	part time
el riesgo	risk	a tiempo completo	full time

◆ **Higher phrases**

Quisiera trabajar en algo relacionado con la informática/los ordenadores.
I'd like a job to do with computers.

Me encantaría ser guía de turismo.
I'd love to be a courier.

Hay muchas ventajas – por ejemplo se puede visitar países diferentes.
There are lots of advantages – for example you can visit different countries.

No me apetece trabajar en una ciudad grande.
I don't fancy working in a big city.

Trabajo a tiempo completo/parcial.
I work full/part time.

CAREERS

◆ **Foundation words**

el actor, la actriz	actor, actress	el/la dentista	dentist
el albañil	bricklayer	el dependiente,	shop assistant
el ama de casa	housewife	la dependienta	
el arquitecto,	architect	el electrista	electrician
la arquitecta		el enfermero,	nurse
el/la artista	artist	la enfermera	
el autor, la autora	author	el fontanero,	plumber
el camarero,	waiter, waitress	la fontanera	
la camarera		el fotógrafo,	photographer
el/la cantante	singer	la fotógrafa	
el carnicero,	butcher	el/la futbolista	footballer
la carnicera		el granjero, la granjera	farmer
el carpintero,	carpenter	el/la guía	(holiday) guide
la carpintera		el/la guardia	policeman,
el cartero, la cartera	postman/woman		policewoman
el cocinero, la cocinera	cook	el hombre de negocios	businessman

27

la mujer de negocios	business woman	el pintor, la pintora	painter
el ingeniero, la ingeniera	engineer	el profesor, la profesora	teacher
el mecánico, la mecánica	mechanic	el programador, la programadora	programmer
el médico, la médica	doctor	el secretario, la secretaria	secretary
el músico, la música	musician		
el obrero, la obrera	labourer	el/la socorrista	lifeguard
el panadero, la panadera	baker	el técnico, la técnica	technician
		el tendero, la tendera	shopkeeper
el peluquero, la peluquera	hairdresser	el vendedor, la vendedora	salesman, sales woman
el piloto, la pilota	pilot		

◆ **Foundation phrases**

Trabajo en una tienda los sábados.	I work in a shop on Saturdays.
Empiezo a las nueve y termino a las cinco.	I start at nine and finish at five o'clock.
Gano tres euros por hora.	I earn three euros per hour.
¿En qué trabajan tus padres?	What do your parents do for a living?
Mi madre es arquitecta y mi padre es ingeniero.	My mother is an architect and my father is an engineer.

What jobs are being advertised?

VENDEDOR/A

precisa
INGENIERO
(ELECTROTECNIA O SIMILAR)

HOTEL ****
Precisa
COCINERO

SECRETARIA
(SEVILLA)

Usted puede **GANAR**
DINERO
Copiando direcciones desde
su casa

◆ Higher level words

el abogado, la abogada	lawyer
el/la agente inmobiliario	estate agent
el alcalde	mayor
el arzobispo	archbishop
la azafata	air-hostess
el basurero/la basurera	refuse collector
el cajero, la cajera	cashier
el camionero, la camionera	lorry driver
el cirujano, la cirujana	surgeon
el/la contable	accountant
el/la chófer	chauffeur
el consultor, la consultora	consultant
el/la contrabandista	smuggler
el decorador, la decoradora	decorator
el diseñador, la diseñadora	designer
el encargado, la encargada	person in charge
el farmacéutico, la farmacéutica	chemist
el/la florista	florist
el funcionario, la funcionaria	civil servant
el/la garajista	garage attendant
el/la gerente	manager
el jardinero, la jardinera	gardener

el/la jefe de grupo	section leader
el marinero, la marinera	sailor
el mozo	porter
el obispo	bishop
el pastor, la pastora	shepherd, shepherdess
el/la periodista	journalist
el político, la política	politician
el propietario, la propietaria	owner
el/la sacerdote	priest
el sastre, la sastra	tailor
el veterinario, la veterinaria	vet
el viticultor, la viticultora	vine grower
el zapatero, la zapatera	shoemaker, cobbler
la princesa	princess
el príncipe	prince
la reina	queen
el rey	king
el primer ministro	Prime Minister
el rango	rank
el desempleo	unemployment
desempleado, en paro	unemployed
estar en paro	to be unemployed
la huelga	strike
el/la huelgista	striker

SE NECESITAN
AZAFATAS
PARA CAMPAÑA PROMOCIONAL
EN TODA ESPAÑA

◆ Higher level phrases

En este momento estoy desempleado.	I'm out of work at the present time.
Mi ambición es ser veterinario.	My ambition is to be a vet.
Para ser cirujano tendré que estudiar medicina.	To be a surgeon I will have to study medicine.

ICT AND COMPUTERS

◆ Foundation words

el ordenador	computer	la internet	internet
el cederom (CD Rom)	CD Rom	la página web	web-site
el correo electrónico	e-mail	la pantalla	screen
el cursor	cursor	el programa	program
el disquete	floppy disk	el ratón	mouse
enviar	to send	el teclado	keyboard
el fax	fax	el videojuego	computer game
la impresora	printer		

◆ Foundation phrases

Tengo un ordenador.	I have a computer.
Creo que es muy útil.	I think it is very useful.
Juego al ordenador todos los días.	I play on my computer every day.
Paso mucho tiempo en internet.	I spend a lot of time on the internet.
Me encantan los videojuegos.	I love computer games.

◆ Higher words

el ordenador portátil	laptop	enviar por fax	to fax
el archivo	file	formatear	to format
archivar	to file	navegar por internet	to surf the net
bajar	to download	el procesador de textos	word-processor
el base de datos	database		
cargar	to load	programar	to program
la clave, la contraseña	password	salvar	to save
editar	to edit	trasvasar	to download
el escáner	scanner	la unidad de disco	disk drive

◆ Higher phrases

Mi ordenador portátil costó €1.800.	My laptop cost €1.800.
En vez de escribir cartas envío correo electrónico a mis amigos.	Instead of writing letters I send e-mail to my friends.
En mi opinión lo más útil de un ordenador es que ahorra tiempo.	In my opinion the most useful thing about a computer is that it saves time.
Está programado para darme información muy rápidamente.	It is programmed to give me information very quickly.

POCKET MONEY AND PART TIME JOBS

◆ Foundation words

el dinero de bolsillo	pocket money	los videojuegos	computer games
la paga	pocket money		
recibir	to receive, get	ayudar	to help
dar	to give	en casa	in the house
ganar	to earn	a mis padres	my parents
gastar	to spend		
ahorrar	to save	trabajar	to work
comprar	to buy	el sábado	on Saturday
los caramelos	sweets	los fines de semana	at weekends
el chocolate	chocolate	en una tienda	in a shop
los discos compactos	CDs	empezar (empiezo),	to start (I start)
los libros	books	comenzar (comienzo)	
las revistas	magazines	terminar	to finish
la ropa	clothes	hacer (hago) de	to babysit
los tebeos	comics	canguro	(I babysit)

◆ Foundation phrases

Mi padre me da seis euros por semana.	My dad gives me six euros a week.
¿Qué haces con tu dinero?	What do you do with your money?
Con mi dinero compro revistas y discos compactos.	With my pocket money I buy magazines and CDs.
Trato de ahorrar un poco también.	I try to save a bit as well.
Trabajo en una tienda el sábado.	I work in a shop on Saturday.
Recibo cinco libras esterlinas por hora.	I get £5 per hour.

◆ Higher words

el maquillaje	make-up	imprescindible	essential
la propina	tip	(las) cosas	essential things
la cuenta bancaria	bank account	imprescindibles	

◆ Sopa de letras

Find the words in the wordsearch.

REY

CURA

JEFE

ACTOR

SASTRE

CHOFER

MEDICO

AGENTE

PILOTO

CARTERA

TECNICO

CAMARERA

MARINERO

INGENIERA

J	M	M	E	R	O	C	A	M	R	A	M
M	E	D	I	T	O	N	G	E	C	E	A
O	D	F	O	C	A	M	E	D	D	O	R
A	C	L	A	G	R	Y	N	I	C	A	I
P	I	U	E	M	E	H	C	I	A	C	N
P	A	N	R	R	I	O	N	H	M	T	E
A	T	E	M	A	N	C	R	O	A	R	R
E	C	R	E	C	E	A	A	S	R	E	O
C	A	T	O	T	G	M	M	J	E	F	E
I	N	S	R	O	N	A	A	T	R	O	S
C	U	A	A	R	I	R	C	P	A	H	C
S	A	S	M	A	R	E	T	R	A	C	A

(Answer on page 109)

32

Public Services

POST

◆ Foundation words

Correos	Post Office	enviar, mandar	to send
el estanco, la tabacalera	tobacconist	el paquete	parcel
el buzón	letter box	la postal, la tarjeta	postcard
la carta	letter	dar	to give
echar una carta	to post a letter	deme	give me
querer (quiero)	to want (I want)	el sello	stamp

◆ Foundation phrases

¿Cuánto cuesta enviar una postal a Inglaterra?	How much does it cost to send a postcard to England?
Deme dos sellos de cincuenta centimos por favor.	Give me two 50 centimos stamps please.
¿Dónde está el buzón por favor?	Where is the post box please?
¿Se venden postales aquí?	Do you sell postcards here?

◆ Higher words

la recogida	collection (post)	remitir	to forward
la próxima recogida	next collection	el correo	mail, post
la última recogida	last collection	correo certificado	registered post
el sobre	envelope	correo urgente	special delivery

THE TELEPHONE

◆ Foundation words

el teléfono	telephone	la guía (telefónica)	telephone directory
el teléfono móvil	mobile phone	la línea	line
telefonear	to phone	marcar	to dial
llamar	to call	el prefijo	area code
la llamada	(phone) call	la ranura	slot
el aparato	handset	el recado	message
la cabina	phone box	dejar un recado	to leave a message
descolgar	to pick up (phone)	sonar	to ring (noise of phone)
colgar	to ring off, hang up	¡Diga!/¡Dígame!	Hello
estar comunicando	to be engaged	Soy yo.	It's me.
el fax	fax	¿De parte (de quién?)	Who's that speaking?
enviar un fax	to fax		

◆ Foundation phrases

¿Cuál es tu número de teléfono?	What's your phone number?
¡Dígame, soy Jeremy!	Hello, Jeremy speaking.
¿Puedo hablar con Ana?	Can I speak to Ana?
Quisiera dejar un recado.	I'd like to leave a message.
No cuelgue por favor.	Hold the line please.
No contestan.	There's no answer.
Está comunicando.	It's engaged.

◆ Higher words

¡al aparato!	speaking!
la conferencia	call
de cobro revertido	reversed charge
el contestador automático	answering machine
equivocarse de número	to get the wrong number
introducir monedas	to put in coins
la tarjeta telefónica	phone card
el tono de marcar	dialing tone

◆ Higher phrases

Lo siento, me he confundido de número.	Sorry, I've got the wrong number.
Dile a María que me llame cuando vuelva, por favor.	Tell Maria to call me when she comes back, please.
Te llaman al teléfono.	You're wanted on the phone.
¿Puedes llamarme mañana a las once?	Can you call me tomorrow at eleven?

THE BANK

◆ Foundation words

el banco	bank
el billete	note
la caja	till
el cajero/la cajera	cashier
el cajero automático	cash dispenser
cambiar	to change
la cantidad	quantity
el cheque, talón	cheque
el cheque de viaje/viajero	traveller's cheque
¿cuánto?	how much?
la cuenta bancaria	bank account
el dinero	money
firmar	to sign
la libra (esterlina)	pound (sterling)
la moneda	coin
necesitar	to need
pagar	to pay
el pasaporte	passport
el euro	euro
por ciento	per cent
la tarjeta de crédito	credit card
la ventanilla	counter (in bank)

◆ Foundation phrases

¿A qué hora se abre el banco?	What time does the bank open?
Quiero cambiar cincuenta libras por favor.	I want to change £50 please.
Firme aquí.	Sign here.
Tengo mi pasaporte.	I have my passport.
Necesito unas monedas también.	I need some coins as well.

◆ Higher words

cobrar	to cash	el talonario (de cheques)	cheque book
la sucursal	branch	la tarjeta bancaria	bank card

◆ Higher phrases

Quisiera cobrar un cheque.	I'd like to cash a cheque.
He perdido mi talonario de cheques.	I've lost my cheque book.
Deme billetes de mil por favor.	Give me one thousand peseta notes please.

 **¿SALE USTED DE VACACIONES?** PODEMOS ORIENTARLE EN TODO LO RELACIONADO CON EL DINERO. **CONSULTENOS.**

LOST PROPERTY OFFICE

◆ Foundation words

la oficina de objetos perdidos	lost property office	el pasaporte	passport
perder	to lose	el collar	necklace
el billetero, la cartera	wallet	el reloj	watch
el bolso	handbag	los pendientes	ear-rings
las gafas	spectacles	la pulsera	bracelet
la maleta	suitcase	la marca	make
la máquina de fotos, la máquina fotográfica	camera	dejar	to leave
		lo/la dejé	I left it
		los/las dejé	I left them
		rellenar	to fill in
el paraguas	umbrella	el formulario	form

◆ Foundation phrases

Perdí una máquina de fotos.	I've lost my camera.
La dejé en el autobús.	I left it on the bus.
Mi monedero es rojo.	My purse is red.
¿Tiene un paraguas verde por favor?	Have you got a green umbrella please?

35

◆ **Higher words**

darse cuenta (de que)	to realise (that)	devolver	to give back
entregar	to hand in	el anillo, la sortija	ring

◆ **Higher phrases**

He perdido una maleta negra de cuero.	I've lost a black leather suitcase.
Creo que la dejé en el aeropuerto.	I think I left it at the airport.
En mi billetero había sesenta euros.	There was 60 euros in my wallet.
¿Ha encontrado un reloj de oro, marca Rolex?	Have you found a gold Rolex watch?
¿Podrían ustedes enviármelo por correo?	Could you post it to me?

ADVERTISING

◆ **Foundation words**

el anuncio	advert	la información	information
el color	colour	la opinión	opinion
el consejo	advice	en mi opinión	in my opinion
el éxito	success	el póster	poster
tener éxito	to be successful	la publicidad	advertising
la foto	photo	recomendar	to recommend
la imagen	image, picture	sugerir	to suggest

◆ **Foundation phrases**

En mi opinión este anuncio es estupendo.	In my opinion this advert is fantastic.
Mi hermano trabaja en publicidad.	My brother works in advertising.
No me gusta nada esta imagen.	I don't like this picture at all.

◆ **Higher words**

aconsejar	to advise	inolvidable	unforgetable
el cartel	poster, placard	el informe	announcement
la cartelera	hoarding, "what's on" section in newspaper	informarse de	to find out about
		interesarse en	to be interested in
		el letrero	sign, notice
impresionante	impressive		

MEDIA

◆ **Foundation words**

el actor	actor	escuchar	to listen to
la actriz	actress	mirar	to watch
el artículo	article	la estrella de cine	movie star

el periódico	newspaper	los dibujos animados	cartoons
poner	to put on, show	el documental	documentary
la radio	radio	el espectáculo	show
la revista	magazine	la lotería	lottery
el satélite	satellite	el sorteo	draw for
TV por satélite	satellite TV		lottery
la televisión	television	el premio gordo	jackpot
la tele	telly	las noticias	news
ver	to see, watch	la película	film
el programa	programme	la serie	serial
la comedia	comedy	la telenovela	soap
los deportes	sports	el telespectador	viewer

◆ Foundation phrases

¿Qué ponen hoy?	What's on today?
A las ocho hay un documental.	There is a documentary at 8 o'clock.
Yo prefiero el fútbol – es más emocionante.	I prefer the football – it's more exciting.
Compro una revista todos los sábados.	I buy a magazine every Saturday.
Leo el periódico antes de ir al colegio.	I read the paper before going to school.

◆ Higher words

abonarse a	to subscribe to	el lector, la lectora	reader
el abono	subscription	las noticias	current affairs, news
acontecer	to happen		
el acontecimiento	event	la obra de teatro	play
la antena parabólica	satellite dish	el papel	the role, part
el argumento	plot	hacer el papel de	to play the part of
el cable	cable TV	el personaje	character
el canal	(TV) channel	la prensa	press
el comentario	commentary, press coverage	presentar	to show (film), put on (play)
el consultorio sentimental	problem page	el programa concurso	games show
		el semanal	weekly (newspaper)
el culebrón	soap		
el diario	daily (newspaper)	el telediario	TV news
estrenar	to show for the first time	el teletexto	teletext
		los titulares	headlines
el estreno	premiere	tratarse de	to be about
filmar	to film	TVE (televisión española)	Spanish television
fotografiar	to photograph		

◆ Higher phrases

¿De qué trata ese libro?	What is that book about?
Trata de una mujer a quién le toca la lotería.	It's about a woman who wins the lottery.

La película me hizo mucha gracia.	I found the film very funny.
¿Qué te pareció la obra?	What did you think of the play?
Una película que presenta a Clint Eastwood en el papel de…	A film featuring Clint Eastwood as…
Según las noticias de hoy hubo un robo en Londres.	According to today's news there was a robbery in London.
En mi opinión Jamie Bell será la estrella del futuro.	In my opinion Jamie Bell will be the star of the future.

TVE–1 (Del 15 al 20 de junio)

JUEVES 14

06.00	CANAL 24 HORAS.	14.30	CORAZON DE PRIMAVERA.	01.30	TELEDIARIO 3.
07.30	TELEDIARIO MATINAL.	15.00	TELEDIARIO 1.	01.55	REYES Y REY.
09.00	LOS DESAYUNOS DE TVE.	16.05	EL SECRETO.	02.45	CORAZON DE PRIMAVERA.
09.50	MARIA EMILIA.	16.45	LA REVANCHA.	03.30	CINE DE MADRUGADA: «un cadáver a los postres».
11.45	SABER VIVIR.	19.00	TOROS: CORRIDA DE LA BENEFICENCIA.		
12.50	ASI SON LAS COSAS.	21.00	TELEDIARIO 2.		
14.00	INFORMATIVO TERRITORIAL.	22.00	ACADEMIA DE BAILE GLORIA.		
		23.30	NUESTRO CINE: «¡se armó el belén!».		

Health

PARTS OF THE BODY

◆ Foundation words

Head:

la cabeza	head	el cuerpo	body
la cara	face	el cuello	neck
el diente, la muela	tooth	el dedo	finger
la garganta	throat	la espalda	back
la lengua	tongue	el estómago	stomach
la nariz	nose	la mano	hand
el oído, la oreja	ear	el pie	foot
el ojo	eye	la pierna	leg

Body:

◆ Higher words

la barbilla	chin	el muslo	thigh
la frente	forehead, brow	el pecho	chest
el corazón	heart	el pulmón	lung
el dedo del pie	toe	los riñones	kidneys
el hígado	liver	el tobillo	ankle
el hombro	shoulder	el vientre, estómago	stomach
los labios	lips	taladrar	to pierce
la mejilla	cheek	la uña	nail
la muñeca	wrist	la voz	voice

ILLNESS

◆ Foundation words

la salud	health	estar resfriado	to have a cold
la enfermedad	illness	tener (tengo)	to have (I have)
doler	to hurt	**tener:**	
me duele (n)…	I've got a bad…	fiebre	to have a temperature
estar (estoy)	to be (I am)	calor	to be hot
bien	well	frío	to be cold
mal	bad	hambre	to be hungry
regular	OK	sed	to be thirsty
enfermo	ill	miedo	to be afraid
herido	hurt, injured	sueño	to be sleepy
mareado	sick	un catarro	to have a cold
cansado	tired	un dolor de cabeza	to have a headache
mejor	better	un dolor de muelas	to have a toothache
peor	worse	la gripe	to have flu

la herida	wound, injury	la quemadura del sol	sunburn
la insolación	sun-stroke	sufrir	to suffer
la picadura	sting, (insect) bite	morir	to die
la quemadura	burn		

◆ Foundation phrases

Me duele la cabeza.	I've got a headache.
Tengo dolor de muelas.	I've got a toothache.
¿Cómo estás?	How are you?
¿Qué te pasa?	What's the matter with you?
¿Estás enfermo?	Are you ill?
Estoy resfriado y tengo tos.	I've got a cold and a cough.

◆ Higher words

abatido	depressed	hacerse daño	to hurt oneself
ahogarse	to drown, suffocate	discapacitado, minusválido	handicapped, disabled
la alergia	allergy	hincharse	to swell
tener alergia a	to be allergic to	hinchado	swollen
el aliento	breath	ir tirando	to get along, manage
el ataque cardíaco	heart attack	la lágrima	tear
el cáncer del pulmón	lung cancer	morder	to bite
cortarse el dedo	to cut one's finger	la regla, el periodo	period
débil	weak	la sangre	blood
desmayarse	to faint, swoon	quejarse de	to complain of
la diarrea	diarrhoea	quemarse la mano	to burn one's hand
sangrar	to bleed	romperse la pierna	to break one's leg
embarazada	pregnant	sentirse bien	to feel fine
tener buena salud	to be in good health	(me siento)	(I feel)
		sentirse mal	to feel ill
tener mala salud	to be in bad health	el SIDA	AIDS
		la silla de ruedas	wheelchair
temblar	to shiver	sudar	to sweat, perspire
el estrés	stress	dolorido, entumecido	sore, numb, stiff
estresado	stressed		
la fiebre del heno	hay-fever	torcerse la muñeca	to twist one's wrist
gravemente herido	seriously injured	el tobillo	one's ankle
la infección	infection		

◆ Higher phrases

Me he hecho daño.	I've hurt myself.
Creo que tengo la pierna rota.	I think I've got a broken leg.
Mi tobillo está muy hinchado.	My ankle is very swollen.
Tengo alergia a la penicilina.	I'm allergic to penicillin.
Cuando se cayó María se torció la muñeca.	When she fell down María twisted her wrist.
Vamos tirando.	We are getting along OK.

REMEDIES AND TREATMENT

◆ Foundation words

la ambulancia	ambulance	la medicina	medicine
la aspirina	aspirin	el médico, la médica	doctor
el comprimido	pill, tablet	la pastilla	tablet
la crema	cream	la receta	prescription
la Cruz Roja	Red Cross	la tirita	(sticky) plaster
la droga	drug	(sala de) urgencias	Casualty Department
el enfermero, la enfermera	nurse	grave	serious
la inyección	injection	urgente	urgent
el jarabe (para la tos)	cough syrup	llamar al médico	to call the doctor
el medicamento	medicine, drug		

◆ Foundation phrases

Quisiera unas aspirinas por favor.	I'd like some aspirins please.
Es urgente.	It's urgent.
Tome dos comprimidos dos veces al día.	Take two tablets twice a day.

◆ Higher words

adelgazar	to slim	empastar	to fill (tooth)
el algodón	cotton wool	el empaste	filling
aliviar	to ease, relieve	engordar	to put on weight
el chequeo	checkup	la escayola	plaster (for broken limb)
el consultorio	doctory's surgery		
la dieta	diet	guardar cama	to stay in bed
estar a dieta	to be on a diet	hacer una dieta	to go on a diet
el ejercicio	exercise	pedir hora/cita	to make an appointment
hacer ejercicio	to take exercise		

perder peso	to lose weight	el transplante	transplant
recuperarse	to recover	el transplante	heart transplant
el régimen	diet	del corazón	
ponerse a régimen	to go on a diet	el tratamiento	treatment
los primeros auxilios	first aid	la venda	bandage
los rayos X	X-rays	el vendaje	dressing
tragar	to swallow	vendar	to bandage

◆ **Higher phrases**

Quisiera pedir hora. Es urgente.	I'd like to make an appointment. It's urgent.
Voy a hacer dieta.	I'm going to go on a diet.
Es preciso que pierda peso.	I need to lose weight.
A mi tío le hicieron un transplante del corazón.	My uncle had a heart transplant.

HEALTHY LIFESTYLE – AM I FIT?

◆ **Foundation words**

aceptable	acceptable	hacer (hago) ejercicio	to do (I do) exercise
el alcohol	alcohol		
sin alcohol	alcohol-free	el humo	smoke
beber	to drink	fumar	to smoke
la bebida	drink	el cigarillo	cigarette
comer	to eat	el tabaco	tobacco
la comida	food, meal	el peligro	danger
el daño	harm	peligroso	dangerous
la droga	drug	saludable, sano	healthy
drogarse	to take drugs	de forma saludable	healthily
el ejercicio	exercise		

◆ **Foundation phrases**

No fumo. Es malo para la salud.	I don't smoke. It's bad for your health.
Hago mucho ejercicio, por ejemplo…	I do a lot of exercise, for example…
En mi opinión drogarse es muy peligroso.	In my opinion to take drugs is very dangerous.

◆ Higher words

el aerobic	aerobics	el fumar pasivo	passive smoking
alcohólico	alcoholic	dejar de fumar	to stop smoking
el alcoholismo	alcoholism	el footing	jogging
el alimento	food	en forma	fit
alimentos bajos en grasas	low-fat foods	mantenerse en forma	to keep fit
la bicicleta de ejercicio	exercise bike	graso	fatty (adj)
las clases de gimnasia	fitness classes	comer grasas	to eat fatty foods
la comida sana	healthy food		
la comida basura	junk food	el riesgo	risk
la comida rápida	fast food	el riesgo para la salud	health hazard
el fumador, la fumadora	smoker		

◆ Higher phrases

No como chocolate porque engorda.   I don't eat chocolate because it's fattening.

Dejé de fumar el año pasado.   I stopped smoking last year.

Hago todo lo posible para mantenerme en forma.   I do my best to keep fit.

Voy a clases de aerobic tres veces a la semana.   I go to aerobics classes three times a week.

Free Time

HOBBIES (GENERAL)

◆ **Foundation words**

el pasatiempo	hobby	la novela	novel
favorito	favourite	la revista	magazine
principal	main	el tebeo	comic
los ratos libres, el	spare time	practicar	to go in for, play
tiempo libre		preferir (prefiero)	to prefer
aburrirse	to get bored		(I prefer)
bailar	to dance	preferido	favourite
el baile	dance	sacar fotos	to take photos
el flamenco	flamenco	salir (salgo)	to go out
coleccionar	to collect		(I go out)
la colección	collection	ver la tele	to watch telly
coser	to sew	visitar	to visit
dibujar	to draw		
diseñar	to design	el ajedrez	chess
encantar	to love	las cartas	cards
me encanta (n)	I love	el juego de cartas	game of cards
gustar	to like	el ordenador	computer
me gusta (n)	I like	el videojuego	computer game
ir (voy)	to go (I go)	el socio	member
jugar (juego)	to play (I play)	ser (soy) socio de	to be (I am)
el juego	game		a member of
el juguete	toy	el club	club
leer	to read	el club de jóvenes	youth club

◆ **Foundation phrases**

¿Qué haces en tus ratos libres?	What do you do in your spare time?
Pues, me gusta mucho leer.	Well, I like reading very much.
Juego en el ordenador.	I play on my computer.
Tengo una colección grande de sellos.	I've got a large collection of stamps.

◆ **Higher words**

la afición	hobby	la costura	sewing
la distracción	pastime,	la aguja	needle
	recreation	el alfiler	pin
la diversión	hobby	la máquina de coser	sewing machine
el ocio	leisure	hacer punto	to knit
el bricolaje	do-it-yourself	distraerse	to amuse oneself
hacer bricolaje	to do DIY	(me distraigo)	(I amuse myself)
el tornillo	screw	el dominó	dominoes
el/la coleccionista	collector	interesar	to interest

el juego de mesa	board game	la preferencia	preference
pintar	to paint	relajarse	to relax, unwind
la pintura	painting	la videocámara	camcorder
predilecto	favourite		

◆ **Higher phrases**

Los juegos de mesa me aburren.	Board games bore me stiff.
Me distraigo viendo la tele.	I find it relaxing to watch TV.
Para relajarme hago crucigramas.	I do crossword puzzles to relax.

S P O R T

◆ **Foundation words**

el deporte	sport	el barco de vela	sailing boat
el/la deportista	sportsman, sportswoman	el windsurf	windsurfing
		montar en bicicleta	to cycle
jugar a	to play (game)	dar un paseo	to go for a walk
el baloncesto	basketball	: en bicicleta	to go for a bike ride
los bolos	10 pin bowling		
el fútbol	football	: en barco	to go for a boat trip
el ping-pong	table tennis		
el tenis	tennis	esquiar	to ski
el tenis de mesa	table tennis	montar a caballo	to go horse-riding
hacer (hago)	to do (I do)		
practicar	to do, practice	nadar	to swim
el aerobic	aerobics	patinar	to skate
el alpinismo	mountain climbing	pescar	to fish
		el partido	match
el atletismo	athletics	el aficionado/la aficionada	fan, supporter
el boxeo	boxing		
el ciclismo	cycling	el equipo	team
la bicicleta/la bici	bike	el jugador/la jugadora	player
la bicicleta de montaña	mountain bike	marcar	to score
la equitación	horse riding	el gol	goal
el esquí	ski-ing	ganar	to win
el footing	jogging	perder (pierdo)	to lose (I lose)
la gimnasia	gymnastics	el resultado	result
el monopatín	skate-boarding	el torneo	competition, tournament
la natación	swimming		
el patinaje	skating	la copa	cup, trophy
los patines	skates	la medalla	medal
la pesca	fishing	el premio	prize
la vela	sailing		

FREE TIME

la bolera	bowling alley	el parque	park
el campo de deportes	playing field	la piscina	swimming baths
el campo de fútbol	football pitch	la pista de hielo	ice rink
la cancha de tenis	tennis court	el polideportivo	sports centre
el estadio	stadium		

◆ Foundation phrases

¿Cuál es tu deporte favorito?	What is your favourite sport?
Me gusta mucho la equitación.	I like horse riding a lot.
Juego al fútbol con mis amigos.	I play football with my friends.
Hago aerobic los fines de semana.	I do aerobics at weekends.
Voy a la piscina en el verano.	I go to the swimming baths in summer.
Tengo una bicicleta de montaña roja.	I've got a red mountain bike.

◆ Higher words

los artes marciales	martial arts	el/la gimnasta	gymnast
el/la atleta	athlete	jugar un partido de	to play a game of
el balón	(large) ball, football	el/la hincha	supporter
		el patinaje	skating
bucear	to dive	:sobre hielo	ice skating
la caña de pescar	fishing rod	:sobre ruedas	roller skating
la carrera	race	la pelota vasca	pelota
la caza	hunting, shooting	la piragua	canoe
		el piragüismo	canoeing
los dardos	darts	la pista de patinar	skating rink
aficionado a los deportes	sporty	remar	to row
		saltar	to jump
empatar	to draw	el salto	jump
entrenarse	to train	el teleférico	cable car
la esgrima	fencing	el telesquí	ski-lift
el espectador	spectator	el/la tenista	tennis player
el esquí acuático	water ski-ing	el volante	shuttlecock
el futbolista	footballer	el voleibol	volley ball

◆ Higher phrases

Me entreno tres veces a la semana.	I train three times a week.
Se me da bien el deporte.	I'm good at sport.
No me atrae el alpinismo.	Mountain climbing doesn't appeal to me.
Soy muy aficionado a la danza contemporánea.	I'm very fond of contemporary dance.

M U S I C

◆ Foundation words

la música	music	el cassette (casete)	cassette player
la música clásica	classical music	el disco	record
la música popular	pop music	el disco compacto	CD
tocar	to play	(compacto)	
	(instrument)	el equipo de música	hi-fi system
el instrumento	instrument	el estéreo	stereo
la batería	drums	el estéreo personal	personal
la flauta	flute		stereo
la guitarra	guitar		
el piano	piano	cantar	to sing
la trompeta	trumpet	la canción	song
		el/la cantante	singer
escuchar	to listen to	el grupo	group
el CD	CD	el concierto	concert
la cassette (casete)	cassette	la discoteca	disco

◆ Foundation phrases

¿Tocas algún instrumento? — Do you play an instrument?
Sí, toco la guitarra. — Yes, I play the guitar.
Mi grupo favorito es Travis. — My favourite group is Travis.

◆ Higher words

el lector de compact disc	CD player	cantar en un coro	to sing in a choir
el compositor	composer	la orquesta	orchestra
el conjunto	music group	silbar	to whistle
el coro	choir	el violín	violin
		el walkman	walkman

◆ Higher phrases

Toco el violín desde hace cuatro años. — I've played the violin for four years.
Me cuesta tocar la trompeta. — I find it difficult to play the trumpet.
Es una canción pegadiza. — It's a catchy song.

47

C I N E M A

◆ Foundation words

el cine	cinema	poner	to show (film)
la película	film	quedar	to remain, be left
la comedia	comedy		
los dibujos animados	cartoons	**Opinions (about films)**	
la película	film	ser	to be
:de amor	love film	aburrido	boring
:de aventuras	adventure film	bueno	good
:de ciencia ficción	science fiction film	divertido	fun, amusing
:romántica	romantic film	emocionante	exciting
:de terror	horror film	espléndido	splendid
:del Oeste	cowboy film	estupendo	great
la taquilla	ticket office	fantástico	fantastic
la entrada	ticket	horrible	awful
sacar una entrada	to get a ticket	fenomenal	great
comenzar, empezar	to start	interesante	interesting
comienza, empieza	it starts	malo	bad
la sesión	performance, show	triste	sad
		llorar	to cry
terminar	to finish	reír	to laugh

◆ Foundation phrases

¿Qué ponen en el cine?	What's on at the cinema?
¿Qué tipo de película es?	What sort of film is it?
¿Cuánto cuestan las entradas?	How much do the tickets cost?
¿Quedan entradas?	Are there any tickets left?
¿A qué hora empieza?	What time does it start?
¿A qué hora termina?	What time does it finish?
La película fue muy emocionante.	The film was very exciting.

◆ Higher words

el argumento	plot	la película policíaca	police/detective film
la cola	queue	el personaje	character (in film/play)
hacer cola	to queue		
la estrella	film star	el público	audience
la butaca	seat	recomendar	to recommend
mayores de	people over the age of	subtitulada, con subtítulos	with subtitles
el papel	role, part	el tema	theme
hacer el papel de	to play the part of	tener lugar	to take place
el héroe	hero	en versión española	Spanish language version
la heroína	heroine		
la película de espionaje	spy film	en versión original	original version
		reírse a carcajadas	to roar with laughter
la película de guerra	war film		

◆ **Higher phrases**

¿Has visto esa película?	Have you seen that film?
¿Qué te pareció?	What did you think of it?
Me gustó muchísimo.	I liked it very much.
La película me hizo mucha gracia.	I found the film very funny.
Fue muy triste – me hizo llorar.	It was very sad. It made me cry.
Me reí a carcajadas.	I laughed till I cried.

OTHER ENTERTAINMENT

◆ Foundation words

el teatro	theatre	el club de la	youth club
la obra	**play**	juventud, el club	
el actor	actor	juvenil	
la actriz	actress	la sala de fiestas	night club
el circo	circus	la corrida	bull fight
el parque	zoo	la plaza de toros	bull ring
zoológico, el zoo		el torero	bull fighter
el elefante	elephant	el toro	bull
el león	lion		
el mono	**monkey**	visitar	to visit
el oso	**bear**	la visita	visit
el tigre	tiger	ver	to see
		vi	I saw
el parque	park	**divertido**	**fun**
el parque de	**funfair**	divertirse	to enjoy oneself
atracciones		(me divierto)	(I enjoy myself)
el parque infantil	playpark	me divertí	I enjoyed myself
el parque temático	theme park	nos divertimos	we enjoyed ourselves
el club	club		

◆ Foundation phrases

El sábado pasado fui al parque de atracciones.	Last Saturday I went to the funfair.
Fue estupendo.	It was great.
Voy al club de la juventud el martes y el viernes.	I go to the youth club on Tuesday and Friday.
Me divierto allí.	I have a good time there.

◆ **Higher words**

el ambiente	atmosphere	pasarlo mal	to have a bad time
el torero	matador, bullfighter	pasarlo bomba, pasarlo de maravilla	to have a great time
matar	to kill	sugerir	to suggest
el payaso	clown	el tiovivo	roundabout, ride
pasarlo bien	to have a good time		

◆ **Higher phrases**

Lo pasamos de maravilla en el parque temático.	We had a great time in the theme park.
La idea de la corrida me repugna.	I find the idea of bullfighting revolting.
¿Por qué no vamos al circo? Será muy interesante.	Why don't we go to the circus? It will be very interesting.
¿Qué opinas de la obra?	What is your opinion of the play?

**Other places of
interest to visit**

Tourism

HOLIDAYS

◆ **Foundation words**

la fiesta	(public) holiday	la casa de vacaciones	holiday house
el día de fiesta, el día festivo	(day) holiday	el chalet	villa
		el club de vacaciones	holiday club
las vacaciones	(period) holidays	el hotel	hotel
las vacaciones de verano	summer holidays	el parador	high class tourist hotel run by the state
las vacaciones de invierno	winter holidays		
		la pensión	boarding house
estar (estoy) de vacaciones	to be (I am) on holiday	el lugar, el sitio	place
		turístico	tourist (adj)
ir (voy) de vacaciones	to go (I go) on holiday	el/la turista	tourist (person)
la excursión	outing, trip	la bolsa	bag
ir (voy) de excursión	to go (I go) on a trip	el equipaje	luggage
		la maleta	suitcase
el intercambio	exchange visit	hacer (hago) las maletas	to pack
viajar	to travel		
el viaje	journey	la crema bronceadora	suntan cream
visitar	to visit	la máquina de fotos	camera
la visita	visit	el pasaporte	passport
pasar	to spend	salir (salgo)	to leave (I leave)
una semana	week	llegar	to arrive
quince días	fortnight	la aduana	customs
un mes	month	el aduanero	customs officer
en	in, at	el aeropuerto	airport
el campo	country (side)	la frontera	frontier
la costa	coast	el vuelo	flight
el extranjero	abroad		
ir al extranjero	to go abroad	las distracciones	things to do
el mar	sea	bailar	to dance
a orillas del mar	at the seaside	bañarse	to bathe, swim
la montaña	mountain	comprar	to buy
la sierra	hills, mountains	el recuerdo	souvenir
la playa	beach	el regalo	present
alojar	to put up	dar (doy) un paseo	to go (I go) for a walk
alojarse	to stay		
el apartamento, piso	apartment	descansar	to rest
el camping	camp site	divertirse (me divierto)	to enjoy oneself (I enjoy myself)
la caravana	caravan		

jugar (juego)	to play (I play)	(See section on sport for other holiday activities)
nadar	to swim	
la piscina	swimming pool	
sacar fotos	to take photos	el/la guía — guide (person)
tomar el sol	to sunbathe	la guía (turística) — guide book
visitar	to visit	el folleto — brochure, pamphlet
el castillo	castle	
el museo	museum	
el lugar de interés	place of interest	quedarse en casa — to stay at home

◆ Foundation phrases

¿Qué haces normalmente durante las vacaciones?	What do you normally do during the holidays?
Por lo general voy de vacaciones con mis padres.	I usually go on holiday with my parents.
Solemos ir a la Costa del Sol durante dos semanas.	We usually go to the Costa del Sol for two weeks.
Tomo el sol y practico el windsurf.	I sunbathe and go windsurfing.
El año pasado fui a Francia.	Last year I went to France.
Viajé en coche con mis amigos.	I travelled by car with my friends.
Me alojé en un hotel.	I stayed in a hotel.
Hizo mucho calor y lo pasé muy bien.	It was very hot and I had a great time.

◆ Higher words

el alojamiento	lodging(s)	la temporada alta	high season
la arena	sand	de temporada baja	off peak
la barca de pesca	fishing boat	tostarse (al sol)	to tan, get brown
broncearse	to get suntanned	la tranquilidad	peace, tranquillity
cama y desayuno	bed and breakfast	tumbarse al sol	to sunbathe
comida y alojamiento	board and lodging	el turismo	tourism
deshacer las maletas	to unpack	las vacaciones organizadas	package holiday
el día festivo	holiday	veranear	to spend the summer (holiday)
la estación de esquí	ski resort		
hospedarse	to put up, stay		
el océano	ocean	el veraneante	holidaymaker
la ola	wave	el veraneo	summer holiday
el parasol	parasol, sunshade	estar de veraneo	to be away on holiday
recorrer	to travel (through)		
el recorrido	journey	volar	to fly

53

◆ Higher phrases

Este año voy a visitar a mi amiga por correspondencia española.	I'm going to visit my Spanish penfriend this year.
Pasaremos una semana en su piso en Barcelona, y una semana en la costa.	We'll spend one week in her flat in Barcelona and one week on the coast.
En realidad prefiero veranear a orillas del mar.	In fact, I prefer to spend the summer holidays at the seaside.
Siempre hay un montón de cosas que hacer.	There's always loads of things to do.
¿Puede informarme sobre las excursiones a Segovia por favor?	Can you give me some information about the trips to Segovia, please?

MARBELLA Alquilo vivienda tres dormitorios, junto playa

MALLORCA bahía de Alcudia, a 200 metros playa, puerto deportivo. Magníficos chalets – dos dormitorios dobles, armarios, cocina amueblada, sótano etc. Terrazas, aparcamiento. Zona residencial, mucho pinar, muchas facilidades.

PLAYA Gandía, particular alquila apartamento lujo, piscina, garaje, vistas mar.

HOTELS

◆ Foundation words

el hotel	hotel	con	with
la pensión	boarding house	el aire acondicionado	air-conditioning
tener	to have	el aparcamiento	car park
¿tiene…?	have you got…?	el ascensor	lift
una habitación	room	el balcón	balcony
: individual	single room	el baño	bath
: con una cama	single room	el cuarto de baño	bathroom
: doble	double room	la ducha	shower
: con dos camas	double room	la lavandería	laundry
libre	free	media pensión	half board
para	for	pensión completa	full board
el adulto	adult	la piscina	swimming
el niño	child		pool

Spanish	English	Spanish	English
la piscina climatizada	heated pool	la llave	key
el restaurante	restaurant	el piso	floor
quedarse	to stay		
para	for	el problema	problem
una noche	one night	quejarse	to complain
dos noches	two nights	no hay	there isn't any
una semana	a week	necesitar	to need
quince días	fortnight	el jabón	soap
de... a...	from... till...	el papel higiénico	toilet paper
desde... hasta...		el secador de pelo	hair dryer
completo	full	la toalla	towel
estar completo	to be full	el ascensor	lift
la recepción	reception	la luz	light
el/la recepcionista	receptionist	no funciona	it doesn't work
reservar	to reserve		
la reserva	reservation	la cuenta	bill
enviar, mandar	to send	pagar la cuenta	to pay the bill
el depósito	deposit	el servicio incluido	service charge included
firmar	to sign		
rellenar	to fill in	la comida	meal
la ficha	registration form	servir	to serve
		el desayuno	breakfast
el apellido	surname	el almuerzo	lunch
el nombre (de pila)	first name	la comida	lunch
el domicilio	residence	la cena	evening meal

◆ **Foundation phrases**

¿Tiene una habitación con ducha?	Have you got a room with a shower?
Quiero pensión completa por favor.	I'd like full-board, please.
Es para dos noches.	It's for two nights.
¿Hay restaurante en el hotel?	Is there a restaurant in the hotel?
¿A qué hora se sirve el desayuno?	What time is breakfast served?
No hay papel higiénico.	There's no toilet paper.
No funciona la ducha/la luz.	The shower/light doesn't work.

HOTEL LAS VEGAS

34 habitaciones nuevas con aire acondicionado, a pie de playa, caja fuerte, doble acristalamiento, totalmente insonorizadas, TV satélite, secadores de pelo en baño de mármol, terraza y vista al mar.

◆ Higher words

con baño adjunto	with an en suite bathroom	el hotel de 4 estrellas	4 star hotel
la bombilla	light bulb	el encargado/la encargada del hotel	hotel keeper
el botones	bellboy	el huésped/la huéspeda	guest
la caja fuerte	safe	mandar por adelantado	to send in advance
la cama de matrimonio	double bed		
(las) camas gemelas	twin beds	particular, privado	private
confirmar	to confirm	a partir de	from (date)
la culpa	blame	la reclamación	(formal) complaint
culpar	to blame		
el doble acristalamiento	double glazing	el libro de reclamaciones	complaints book
fastidiar	to annoy, bother	el servico de habitaciones	room service
enfadarse	to get cross	todo incluido	all inclusive

◆ Higher phrases

Nos ha fastidiado las vacaciones.	It ruined our holidays.
Le ruego me mande una tarifa de precios.	Could you please send me a price list.
Quiero quejarme al gerente.	I want to complain to the manager.
Quisiera reservar una habitación para tres noches en su establecimiento.	I should like to reserve a room for three nights in your establishment.

Benidorm

La bahía de Benidorm está formada por dos maravillosas playas orientadas al Sur, con un total de siete kilómetros de aguas tranquilas y finas arenas. Su limpieza y escasa profundidad permiten a niños y mayores gozar sin limitaciones de la jornada playera.

Palamós.—11.500 habitantes. Situada casi en el centro geográfico de la Costa Brava, reúne los atractivos propios de una población activa con los de una estación turística. Excelentes instalaciones portuarias hacen de Palamós centro de estas actividades deportivas. Sus playas, de casi un kilómetro, unidas a sus acantilados y bellos parajes hacen de esta villa un centro animado y cosmopolita. Museo (colecciones de moluscos, pintura moderna y cerámica antigua).

Llafranch.—Pequeña aldea formada por un conjunto de casas blancas que descienden desde la montaña al mar; hermosa bahía, con paseo maritimo; playa de excelente arena, de una extensión de medio kilómetro. Al lado de la misma se halla la montaña, faro y ermita de San Sebastián, desde donde se divisa una de las más bellas panorámicas. Puerto deportivo.

C A M P I N G

◆ Foundation words

el camping	camp site	la lavandería	laundry
acampar	**to camp**	el parque infantil	play area
el adulto	adult	la recepción	reception
el árbol	tree	el restaurante	restaurant
la caravana	caravan	los servicios	toilets
ir (voy) de camping	to go (I go) camping		
el niño/la niña	child	**el equipo**	**equipment**
el sitio	room, space	el abrebotellas	bottle opener
la sombra	shade	el abrelatas	tin opener
la tienda	tent	las cerillas	matches
		la pila	battery
los servicios	**facilities**	el sacacorchos	cork-screw
el agua potable	drinking water	el saco de dormir	sleeping bag
los aseos	toilets		
(caballeros)	(men)	**las reglas**	**rules, regulations**
(señoras)	(women)	prohibir	to prohibit
los baños	wash area	se prohibe,	you are not
el bar	bar	prohibido	allowed to
la cafetería	café	encender	to light
la comida para llevar	take away meal	el fuego	fire
las duchas	showers	tirar	to throw
		la basura	rubbish

◆ Foundation phrases

¿Hay sitio en el cámping?	Have you got any room on the campsite?
¿Cuánto cuesta por noche/por persona?	How much does it cost per night/person?
Somos cuatro: dos adultos y dos niños.	There are four of us: two adults and two children.
Prefiero estar en la sombra.	I prefer to be in the shade.
¡No tirar basura!	No litter!

ABIERTO TODO EL AÑO

♣ Agua Potable

DUCHAS

Velocidad máxima 10 km/h

¡Se prohibe encender fuego!

◆ Higher words

la alimentación	food	montar una tienda	to put up a tent
la barbacoa	barbecue	la navaja	penknife
el/la campista	camper	la norma	rule
cumplir	to comply with	la parcela	plot of land, pitch
la dirección	management	la plaza	space
el enchufe	power point	recordar	to remind
equipar	to equip	respetar	to respect
equipado	equipped	rogar	to request
el hornillo de gas	gas stove	vigilar	to keep an eye on
la linterna eléctrica	torch	vigilado	supervised

CAMPING MUNICIPAL DE CINTRUENIGO

CINTRUENIGO   TEL. (948) 81 24 77

■ **SITUACION**
La villa de Cintruénigo cuenta con más de 5.000 habitantes y ofrece al turista todos los servicios para hacer más cómoda su estancia. El cámping se encuentra situado a 200 m. del núcleo urbano. Acceso: N-113 Soria-Pamplona. Comarcal N-160 Tudela-Fitero, a 18 Kms. de Tudela, capital de la Ribera.

Capacidad: 200 Plazas.   Categoría: 2ª

◆ Higher phrases

¿Puede reservarme un espacio para dos días en su camping por favor?	Could you please reserve me a place for two days on your campsite?
Está estrictamente prohibido cambiar de emplazamiento sin permiso.	It is strictly prohibited to change site without permission.
¿Dónde deberíamos montar nuestra tienda?	Where should we pitch our tent?
¿Se pueden alquilar bicicletas?	Can you hire bikes?

YOUTH HOSTEL

◆ **Foundation words**

el albergue juvenil	youth hostel	el salón	lounge
pasar las vacaciones	to go youth	alquilar	to hire
en albergues juveniles	hostelling	la manta	blanket
la cocina	kitchen	el saco de dormir	sleeping bag
el comedor	dining room	la tarifa	price list
el dormitorio	bedroom, dormitory		

◆ **Higher words**

el guardián, la guardiana	warden	la tarjeta de socio	membership card
la sábana	sheet		

◆ **Crucigrama: en el hotel**

1 ¿Dónde está la **X**? Quiero nadar.
2 Quiero una habitación **X**.
3 No hay baño pero hay una **X**.
4 ¿Cómo me voy a lavar? No hay **X**.
5 ¿A qué hora se sirve el **X**?
6 Es fácil subir a la habitación en el **X**.
7 Trabaja en la recepción.
8 El camarero trabaja en el **X** del hotel.
9 ¿Quiere **X** completa?
10 ¿Cuánto cuesta por **X**?
11 Necesitas una **X** para entrar en la habitación.

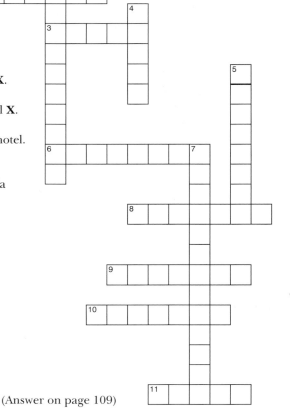

(Answer on page 109)

Social Activities

MEETING PEOPLE (GREETINGS)

◆ Foundation words

¡hola!	hello	¿y usted?	and you? (polite)
¡buenos días!	good morning, good day	adiós	goodbye!
		¡hasta la vista!	see you! so long!
¡buenas tardes!	good afternoon, good evening	¡hasta luego!	see you later!
		¡hasta mañana!	see you
¡buenas noches!	good evening, good night	¡hasta pronto!	see you soon!
		presentar	to introduce
señor	sir	saludar	to greet
señora	madam	el amigo	friend
señorita	miss	el compañero	companion
¿qué tal?	how's things?	¡encantado!	pleased to meet you!
¿qué hay? ¿qué pasa?	what's up?		
¿cómo estás?	how are you? (familiar)	¡mucho gusto! ¡tanto gusto!	pleased to meet you!
¿cómo está usted?	how are you? (polite)	¡el gusto es mío!	the pleasure is mine!
(muy) bien	(very) well	¡bienvenido!	welcome!
gracias	thank you	conocer	to know (person), be acquainted with
estar (estoy) bien	to be (I am) well		
estar (estoy) fatal	to be (I am) awful	(conozco)	(I know)
		despedirse de (me despido)	to say goodbye to (I say goodbye)
estar (estoy) regular	to be (I am) OK		
¿y tú?	and you? (familiar)	la hospitalidad	hospitality

◆ Foundation phrases

¡Hola! ¿Qué tal?	Hello! How are you?
Muy bien, gracias. ¿Y tú?	Very well thank you. And you?
Quiero presentarte a mi hermano.	I'd like to introduce my brother.
¡Encantado de conocerle!	Pleased to meet you!
¡Adiós! ¡Hasta mañana!	Goodbye! See you tomorrow!

◆ Higher words

¡cuánto tiempo sin verte!	long time no see!	acogedor	welcoming, friendly
acoger, dar la bienvenida a	to welcome	dar la mano a	to shake hands with
		reconocer	to recognise

60

ARRANGING A MEETING
(ACCEPTING AND DECLINING)

◆ Foundation words

la cita	date, appointment	de nada	not at all, don't mention it
la invitación	invitation		
invitar	to invite	me gustaría (mucho)	I should like to (very much)
ir (voy)	to go (I go)		
querer (quiero)	to want (I want)	depende	it depends
¿quieres ir?	do you want to go?	es posible	it's possible
¿te gustaría ir?	would you like to go?	posiblemente	possibly
vamos	let's go	probable	probable
vamos a ver	let's see	probablemente	probably
verse	to meet	quizá(s)	perhaps
quedar (+ time)	to meet (at … o'clock)	no sé	I don't know
¿a qué hora?	at what time?	creo que no	I don't think so
¿cuándo?	when?	no	no
¿dónde?	where?	por desgracia, desafortunadamente, desgraciadamente	unfortunately
tener ganas de	to feel like		
sí	yes		
de acuerdo	OK	es imposible	it's impossible
¡buena idea!	good idea!	no es posible	it's not possible
claro	of course	no puedo	I can't
con mucho gusto	with pleasure	¿por qué (no)?	why (not)?
creo que sí	I think so	porque	because
(muchas) gracias	thank you (very much)	lo siento (mucho)	I'm (very) sorry

◆ Foundation phrases

¿Quieres ir al cine?	Do you want to go to the cinema?
Sí, me gustaría mucho.	Yes, I'd like to very much.
Vamos a la piscina.	Let's go to the swimming baths.
¿A qué hora nos vemos?	What time shall we meet?
Lo siento. Esta noche no puedo.	I'm sorry. I can't tonight.

◆ Higher words

¡en absoluto!	no way! certainly not!	disculpar	to excuse
acaso	perhaps	¡discúlpeme!	I'm sorry!
agradecer	to thank	encantar	to love
apetecer	to fancy (doing something)	me es igual	it's all the same to me
		¡no hay de qué!	don't mention it!
citarse, quedar con	to arrange to meet someone	no importa	it doesn't matter
		tal vez	perhaps
dar las gracias	to thank	ya veremos	we'll see (about that)

61

◆ Higher phrases

¿Te apetece ir a la bolera?	Do you fancy going to the bowling alley?
Quedamos para las ocho.	Let's meet at 8 o'clock.
¿Qué te parece?	What do you think?
Creo que es una buena idea.	I think it's a good idea.
Me encantaría verte.	I would love to see you.

EXCLAMATIONS

◆ Foundation words

¡qué asco!	how revolting!	¡buena suerte!	good luck!
¡qué bien!	great! fantastic!	¡caramba! ¡Dios mío!	good gracious!
¡qué horror!	how awful!	¡madre mía!	oh dear! good heavens!
¡qué lástima!	what a pity!		
¡qué pena!	what a shame!	¡ni hablar!	no way!
¡qué sorpresa!	what a surprise!	¡ya lo creo!	you bet!
¡qué va!	rubbish! nonsense!		

◆ Higher words

¡vaya sorpresa!	what a surprise!

SPECIAL EVENTS AND FESTIVALS

◆ Foundation words

celebrar	to celebrate	la fiesta	festival
la boda	wedding	el día festivo	holiday
el cumpleaños	birthday	el Año Nuevo	New Year
la luna de miel	honeymoon	el día de Año Nuevo	New Year's Day
el santo	saint's day	el Carnaval	Carnival (traditional period of fun, feasting and partying preceding Lent)
la fiesta	party		
la fiesta de sorpresa	surprise party		
organizar una fiesta	to have a party		
la fiesta de cumpleaños	birthday party	el Día de Reyes	6th January (when children in Spain get their Christmas presents)
la tarta de cumpleaños	birthday cake		
		la Navidad	Christmas
dar (doy)	to give (I give)	la Pascua	Easter
recibir	to receive, get	la Semana Santa	Holy Week
el regalo	present	el Viernes Santo	Good Friday
la tarjeta	card	la misa	Mass

la misa del gallo	Midnight Mass	¡qué lo pase(s) bien!	have a good time!
¡enhorabuena!	congratulations!		
¡felicidades!	best wishes, happy birthday!	la religión	religion
¡Feliz año nuevo!	Happy New Year!	católico	Catholic
¡Feliz cumpleaños!	Happy birthday!	cristiano	Christian
¡Feliz Navidad!	Happy Christmas!	judío	Jewish
¡Felices Pascuas!	Merry Christmas!	protestante	Protestant
¡Feliz Santo!	Happy Saint's Day!		

◆ Foundation phrases

Mañana es mi cumpleaños.	Tomorrow it's my birthday.
Cumpliré quince años.	I'll be 15.
Voy a organizar una fiesta.	I'm going to have a party.
Recibí muchos regalos este año.	I got a lot of presents this year.
Tengo mucha suerte ¿verdad?	I'm very lucky, aren't I?

◆ Higher words

el festejo	celebration	las uvas de la suerte	12 grapes eaten on New Year's Eve, one on each chime, supposed to bring luck
la festividad	festivity		
religioso	religious		
hindú	Hindu		
musulmán	Muslem		
el Día de Todos los Santos	All Saints' Day		
Pentecostés	Whit(sun)	la tertulia	evening gathering, party
los fuegos artificiales	fireworks	la verbena	open air dance, celebration
el roscón de Reyes	traditional cake eaten on 6th January		

The International World

COUNTRIES

◆ **Foundation words**

el mundo	world	Australia	Australia
el país	country	China	China
Gran Bretaña	Great Britain	chino/a	Chinese
británico	British	Japón	Japan
Escocia	Scotland	japonés, japonesa	Japanese
escocés, escocesa	Scottish	los Estados Unidos	United States
Gales	Wales	norteamericano/a	American
galés, galesa	Welsh	EE. UU.	US(A)
Inglaterra	England	Nueva York	New York
inglés, inglesa	English	Canadá	Canada
Irlanda	Ireland	canadiense	Canadian
Irlanda del Norte	Northern Ireland		
		América del Sur	South America
irlandés, irlandesa	Irish	americano/a,	South American
Londres	London	sudamericano/a	
		Argentina	Argentina
Europa	Europe	Bolivia	Bolivia
europeo	European	Chile	Chile
Alemania	Germany	Colombia	Colombia
alemán, alemana	German	Ecuador	Ecuador
Austria	Austria	Méjico (México)	Mexico
Bélgica	Belgium	mejicano/a, mexicano/a	Mexican
belga	Belgian	Paraguay	Paraguay
Bruselas	Brussels	Perú	Peru
Dinamarca	Denmark	Venezuela	Venezuela
España	Spain	la provincia	province
español, española	Spanish	Andalucía	Andalusia
Francia	France	andaluz, andaluza	Andalusian
francés, francesa	French	Castilla	Castile
Grecia	Greece	castellano/a	Castilian
griego/a	Greek	Cataluña	Catalonia
Holanda	Holland	catalán	Catalan
holandés, holandesa	Dutch	Galicia	Galicia
Italia	Italy	gallego/a	Galician
italiano/a	Italian		
Portugal	Portugal	los Andes	Andes
portugués, portuguesa	Portuguese	los Pirineos	Pyrenees
Rusia	Russia	el Canal de la Mancha	English Channel
ruso/a	Russian		
Suecia	Sweden	el Mediterráneo	Mediterranean Sea
sueco/a	Swedish		
Suiza	Switzerland		
suizo/a	Swiss		

◆ Foundation phrases

Mi madre es escocesa.	My mother is Scottish.
¿De qué nacionalidad eres?	What nationality are you?
Soy inglés.	I'm English.
¿Has visitado España?	Have you been to Spain.
No, pero me gustaría ir.	No, but I would like to go.

◆ Higher words

el Reino Unido	United Kingdom	vasco/a	Basque
Edimburgo	Edinburgh	danés, danesa	Danish
el Támesis	river Thames	Marruecos	Morocco
las Baleares	Balearic Islands	el Atlántico	Atlantic Ocean
las Canarias	Canary Islands	las Naciones Unidas	United Nations
el País Vasco	Basque Country	emigrar	to emigrate

SOCIAL ISSUES

◆ Foundation words

el problema	problem	drogarse	to take drugs
la sociedad	society	el parado	unemployed person
el alcohol	alcohol		
alcohólico	alcoholic (adj)	en paro	unemployed
borracho	drunk	estar en paro	to be unemployed
emborracharse	to get drunk		
el divorcio	divorce	el crimen, el delito	crime
fumar	to smoke	el criminal	criminal
el cigarillo	cigarette	molestar	to annoy, bother
el tabaco	tobacco		
el humo	smoke	el revólver	gun, revolver
dañar	to harm, damage	robar	to steal
		el robo	robbery
el daño	harm, damage	la policía	police
el peligro	danger	detener	to arrest
peligroso	dangerous		
la droga	drug	(See also chapter on Health – Am I Fit?)

◆ Foundation phrases

Mi hermano está en paro.	My brother is unemployed.
Prefiero las bebidas no alcohólicas.	I prefer non-alcoholic drinks.
Mis padres fuman pero yo no.	My parents smoke but I dont't.
No quiero emborracharme.	I don't want to get drunk.

◆ Higher words

asesinar	to murder	el inmigrante	immigrant
el asesino	murderer	el ladrón	thief
amenazar	to threaten	llevarse bien/mal con	to get on well/badly with
la amenaza	threat		
el atraco	hold up, robbery, mugging	el malhechor/la malhechora	criminal
la batalla	battle	la manifestación	demonstration
la cárcel	prison	manifestarse	to hold a rally, demonstrate
la comunidad	community		
el crimen	crime	la molestia	bother, trouble
la culpa	blame	la muerte	death
culpar, echar la culpa	to blame	los países en vías de desarrollo	developing countries
culpable	guilty		
el delito	crime	pelear	to fight
el desempleo	unemployment	la pelea	fight
desempleado	unemployed	la pistola	pistol, gun
discutir	to argue	el prejuicio	prejudice
la discusión	argument	el prisionero	prisoner
disputar	to dispute	probar una droga	to try a drug
la disputa	dispute	protestar	to protest
el drogadicto	drug addict	el público	public
enfadarse, enojarse	to get angry	el ratero	pick-pocket, shoplifter
engañar	to deceive, trick		
escupir	to spit	el refugiado	refugee
entenderse	to understand each other, get on	refugiarse	to flee, take refuge
equivocarse	to make a mistake	reñir	to fall out, quarrel
fastidiar	to annoy, bother	rescatar	to ransom
el gamberro	vandal, hooligan	el rescate	ransom
el gamberrismo	vandalism	secuestrar	to kidnap
el gobierno	government	el secuestro	kidnapping
golpear	to hit	sin hogar, sin techo	homeless
el golpe	blow	el sindicato	union
grosero	rude	socorrer	to help, aid
la guerra	war	el socorro	help, aid
la huelga	strike	el tercer mundo	third world
el/la huelgista	striker	el terrorista	terrorist
hurtar	to steal	la violencia	violence
el hurto en tiendas	shoplifting	la violencia callejera	street violence

◆ **Higher phrases**

¿Le molesta que fume?	Do you mind if I smoke?
Los camioneros se declararon en huelga.	The lorry drivers came out on strike.
Hubo una pelea delante del estadio.	There was a fight in front of the stadium.
En mi opinión fumar es cosa de bobos.	In my opinion smoking is a mug's game.
¡No prueben las drogas!	Don't try drugs!
Los cigarillos me dan asco.	Cigarettes disgust me.

ENVIRONMENTAL ISSUES

◆ **Foundation words**

la ecología	ecology	la campaña	campaign
ecológico	ecological	controlar	to control
el medio ambiente	environment	evitar	to avoid
el mundo	world	preocuparse	to worry
el planeta	planet	protestar	to protest
el aire	air	proteger	to protect
el mar	sea	recomendar	to recommend
la tierra	earth, land	el recurso	resource
la selva	forest	respetar	to respect
amenazar	to threaten	salvar	to save
arruinar	to ruin		
la basura	rubbish	el atasco, el embotellamiento	traffic jam
del hogar	household	la circulación, el tráfico	traffic
la causa	cause	la gasolina (sin plomo)	(unleaded) petrol
causar	to cause	el peatón	pedestrian
la contaminación	contamination	peatonal	pedestrian (adj)
contaminar	to contaminate	la zona peatonal	pedestrian precinct
el desastre	disaster	el vehículo	vehicle
desastroso	disastrous	la urbanización	urbanization
la destrucción	destruction	la vivienda	housing
destruir	to destroy		
estropear	to ruin		
la polución, la contaminación	pollution		
ahorrar	to save (money)		
ayudar	to help		

◆ **Foundation phrases**

Hay demasiada polución.	There is too much pollution.
Tenemos que respetar los animales.	We have to respect animals.
La contaminación amenaza el planeta.	Contamination is threatening the planet.
¿Qué podemos hacer para ayudar?	What can we do to help?

◆ Higher words

abandonar	to abandon	los gases de escape	exhaust fumes
aprovecharse de	to take advantage of	el gasóleo	diesel (oil)
		gotear	to leak
arder	to burn	imprescindible	essential
la avalancha	avalanche	intervenir	to intervene
la ballena	whale	la inundación	flood
el calentamiento del planeta	global warming	el lodo	mud
		la lluvia ácida	acid rain
la capa del ozono	ozone layer	la marea negra	oil slick
casero	household	morir de hambre	to starve
la central nuclear	nuclear power station	la naturaleza	nature
		nuclear	nuclear
colaborar	to collaborate	la pérdida	loss
el daño	harm	preocuparse	to be concerned
dañar	to harm	prescindir de	to get rid of
dañino, dañoso	harmful	químico	chemical
el delfín	dolphin	reasegurar	to reassure
los desechos	waste products	reciclar	to recycle
los desperdicios	rubbish, refuse	los recursos naturales	natural resources
el efecto invernadero	greenhouse effect		
		resolver	to resolve
la electricidad	electricity	respirar	to breathe
las emisiones	emissions	la selva tropical	rainforest
la escasez	shortage	la sequía	drought
la especie en peligro de extinción	endangered species	solucionar	to solve
		el suceso	event
la falta	lack	suceder	to happen
la falta de lluvia	lack of rain	la suciedad	dirt, filth
faltar	to lack	el terremoto	earthquake
el fuego	fire	venirse abajo	to cave in, collapse
fundir	to melt		
el gas	gas		

◆ Higher phrases

Me interesan mucho los asuntos ecológicos.

I'm very interested in environmental issues.

Creo que la contaminación es un problema mundial.

I think that pollution is a world-wide problem.

Me preocupo mucho por las especies en peligro.

I'm very concerned about endangered species.

Es preciso que todos los países colaboren más para solucionar el problema del agujero en la capa del ozono.

It's necessary for all countries to collaborate more to solve the problem of the hole in the ozone layer.

68

THE NATURAL ENVIRONMENT
(COUNTRYSIDE)

◆ Foundation words

el campo	country(side)	la montaña	mountain
la aldea	village	el paisaje	countryside
el árbol	tree	el pájaro	bird
el arbusto	bush	la planta	plant
el bosque	wood	el río	river
el campo	field	la roca	rock
cultivar	to cultivate, grow	la selva	forest
la flor	flower	la sierra	mountain range
la granja	farm	el toro	bull
la hierba	grass	el tractor	tractor
el lago	lake	la vaca	cow
		el valle	valley

◆ Foundation phrases

Mi tío vive en una aldea en el campo. My uncle lives in a village in the country.
El paisaje es muy pintoresco. The countryside is very picturesque.

◆ Higher words

General

el acantilado	cliff	el muro	wall
agrícola	agricultural	el prado	meadow
el apoyo	well	el sendero	path
el arroyo	stream	el seto, la valla	fence
la bahía	bay	la vendimia	grape harvest
el campesino	peasant	la viña	vine, vineyard
campestre	rural	el viñedo	vineyard
la caza	hunting	el/la vinicultor/a, el/la viticultor/a	wine grower
el cerro, la colina	hill	la vinicultura, la viticultura	wine growing, wine producing
la cosecha	harvest	la zona para merendar	picnic area
cosechar	to harvest		
la cueva	cave	**Flora and Fauna (Animals, Birds, Insects, Trees)**	
la cumbre	peak, summit	el burro	donkey
el embalse	reservoir	la cabra	goat
la flor silvestre	wild flower	el cerdo	pig
el granjero	farmer	la culebra	snake
el huerto	orchard	la oveja	sheep
laborable	workable	la rana	frog
el labrador	farm worker	el zorro	fox
el llano, la llanura	plain		
el monte	mountain, hill		

69

el búho	owl	el mosquito	mosquito
la gallina	hen		
el gallo	cockerel	el álamo	poplar tree
el ganso	goose	el manzano	apple tree
el pato	duck	la palmera	palm tree
		el peral	pear tree
la abeja	bee	el pino	pine tree
la avispa	wasp	el roble	oak tree
la mosca	fly	el tronco	trunk

◆ **Higher phrases**

Aquí no cosechan sino patatas.	The only thing they grow here is potatoes.
Tenemos una granja lechera.	We have a dairy farm.
En mi opinión la caza del zorro es cruel.	In my opinion fox-hunting is cruel.

THE WEATHER

◆ **Foundation words**

el tiempo	weather	el clima	climate
¿qué tiempo hace?	what is the weather like?	caluroso	hot
		el hielo	ice
hace…	it is…	la lluvia	rain
:calor	hot	mejorarse	to improve
:fresco	cool	la nieve	snow
:frío	cold	la nube	cloud
:mal tiempo	bad weather	el pronóstico del tiempo	weather forecast
:sol	sunny		
:viento	windy	la temperatura	temperature
está despejado	the sky is clear	alto	high
está nublado	it is cloudy	bajo	low
hay…	it is…	máximo	maximum
:hielo	icy	mínimo	minimum
:niebla	foggy	el grado	degree
:tormenta	stormy	bajo cero	below zero
		la tempestad, la tormenta	storm
llover	to rain	el viento	wind
llueve	it rains	fuerte	strong
nevar	to snow	ligero	light
nieva	it snows	soplar	to blow

70

◆ Foundation phrases

Hoy hace much frío.	Today it's very cold.
Llueve mucho en Manchester.	It rains a lot in Manchester.
Mañana va a hacer sol.	Tomorrow it's going to be sunny.
¡Qué calor!	How hot it is!
Temperaturas bajas en toda la región.	Low temperatures in all the region.
El pronóstico para hoy, lunes.	The forecast for today, Monday.

◆ Higher words

el aguacero	(heavy) shower
el amanecer	dawn
el atardecer	dusk
arder	to burn
ardiente	burning
bochornoso	close, sultry
el boletín meteorológico	weather forecast
la borrasca	storm
brillar	to shine
la brisa	breeze
calentar	to warm, heat
caluroso	warm
sin cambio	unchanged
el chubasco	downpour, squall
el claro	clearing, break in the clouds
débil	weak, light
descender	to drop (temperature)
despejar	to brighten up
diurno	daytime
elevado	high
empeorar	to get worse
la escarcha	frost
estable	constant
la estrella	star
el extremo	extreme
extremadamente	extremely
el granizo	hail
helar	to freeze
húmedo	damp
llover a cántaros	to pour
lloviznar	to drizzle
la luna	moon
lluvioso	rainy, wet
la mejora	improvement
mejorar	to improve
moderado	moderate
mojado	soaked
mojarse	to get wet
:hasta los huesos	to get soaked to the skin
la neblina	mist
con neblina	misty
la nevada	snowfall
la nubosidad	cloudiness
nuboso	cloudy, overcast
el período de sol	sunny period
la precipitación	rainfall
la puesta del sol	sunset
el relámpago	lightning
el riesgo (de)	risk (of)
la salida del sol	sunrise
secar	to dry
seco	dry
sin nubes	cloudless, clear
soleado	sunny
subir	to rise (temperature)
templado	mild
la temporada	spell
tormentoso	stormy
tronar	to thunder
el trueno	thunder
variar	to vary, change
variable	changeable
ventoso	windy
la visibilidad	visibility

◆ **Higher phrases**

La lluvia nos mojó a todos.	The rain soaked us all.
¡Estoy helado!	I'm frozen!
Mañana hará calor en el sur pero lloverá en la costa.	Tomorrow it will be hot in the south but it will rain on the coast.

 # Nubes y lluvias casi generales

Nuboso salvo en el tercio norte. Chubascos en el sur y sureste y nieve entre los 1.300 a 1.500 metros. Las temperaturas sin cambios salvo Canarias donde descenderán.

GALICIA. — (Máxima: 14/Mínima: -1). Nuboso con lluvias débiles. Temperaturas estables.

ASTURIAS, CANTABRIA Y PAIS VASCO. — (Máxima: 18/Mínima: 3). Poco nuboso salvo nubes medias y altas. Temperaturas estables.

CASTILLA Y LEON. — (Máxima: 15/Mínima: -1). Nuboso con chubascos dispersos. Temperaturas estables.

LA RIOJA, NAVARRA Y ARAGON. — (Máxima: 14/Mínima: 0). Nevadas en los Pirineos y Sistema Ibérico. Temperaturas estables.

CATALUÑA. — (Máxima: 15/Mínima: 4). Nuboso con chubascos en el litoral. Temperaturas diurnas más bajas.

CASTILLA-LA MANCHA Y EXTREMADURA. — (Máxima: 15/Mínima: 3). Muy nuboso con nieve sobre los 1.500 metros. Temperaturas estables.

COMUNIDAD VALENCIANA. — (Máxima: 16/Mínima: 6). Muy nuboso. Temperaturas estables.

BALEARES. — (Máxima: 15/Mínima: 2). Nuboso con lluvias moderadas. Temperaturas estables.

ANDALUCIA. — (Máxima: 17/Mínima: 7). Más nuboso en la mitad occidental. Temperaturas estables.

MURCIA. — (Máxima: 15/Mínima: 8). Muy nuboso con lluvias. Temperaturas estables.

CANARIAS. — (Máxima: 22/Mínima: 14). Nuboso en el norte. Temperaturas bajas.

Home Town

PLACES IN TOWN

◆ **Foundation words**

el pueblo	(small) town	el garaje	garage
la ciudad	town, city	el hospital	hospital
		la iglesia	church
el aeropuerto	airport	el mercado	market
el albergue juvenil	**youth hostel**	el monumento	monument
el ayuntamiento	**town hall**	el museo	museum
el banco	bank	la oficina de turismo	tourist office
la biblioteca	**library**	**el palacio**	**palace**
la bolera	**bowling alley**	el parque	park
la cafetería	cafe	**el paso de peatones**	**pedestrian**
el castillo	castle		**crossing**
la catedral	cathedral	la piscina	swimming baths
el centro comercial	**shopping centre**	la plaza	square
el cine	cinema	: mayor	main square
el colegio	school	: de toros	bull ring
la comisaría	**police station**	el polideportivo	leisure centre
correos	the post office	el puente	bridge
la discoteca	**disco**	el puerto	port
el edificio	**building**	el restaurante	restaurant
la estación	station	el supermercado	supermarket
: de autobuses	bus station	la tienda	shop
: de servicio	service station		
el estadio	stadium		
la fuente	**fountain**	(for different types of shop see chapter	
la galería de arte	**art gallery**	on Shopping and Eating)	

◆ **Foundation phrases**

¿Qué hay en tu ciudad?	What is there in your town?
Pues, hay un banco, un cine, un hospital y muchas tiendas.	Well, there is a bank, a cinema, a hospital and a lot of shops.
Mi pueblo es bastante aburrido.	My town is quite boring.
En Durham hay una catedral y un castillo.	In Durham there is a cathedral and a castle.
Muchos turistas vienen aquí en el verano.	A lot of tourists come here in the summer.

◆ Higher words

el acueducto	aqueduct	las murallas	(city) walls
la bodega	wine cellar	la pista de hielo	ice rink
el campo de golf	golf course	la pista de patinar	skating rink
la cervecería	bar, public house	la torre	tower
la estatua	statue	la zona peatonal	pedestrian precinct
la gasolinera	petrol station	datar de	to date back to

◆ Higher phrases

En esta ciudad no nos falta nada. — There is nothing we need in this town.

Las diversiones para los jóvenes son muy limitadas. — The entertainment for young people is very limited.

ASKING THE WAY (DIRECTIONS)

◆ Foundation words

perdone/por favor	excuse me/please	entre	between
señor	sir	al final de	at the end of
señora	madam	al lado de	next to
señorita	miss	lejos de	far from
¿dónde está…?	where is…?	a la izquierda	on the left
¿hay un/una… por aquí?	is there a… near here?	a la derecha	on the right
¿para ir al/a la…?	how do I get to the…?	a mano izquierda/derecha	on the left/right hand side
¿está cerca?	is it near?	en la esquina	on the corner
¿está lejos?	is it far?	bajar	to go down
está	it is	baje	go down
a cinco kilómetros	five kilometres away	subir	to go up
a doscientos metros	two hundred metres away	suba	go up
		la calle	street
a dos minutos	two minutes away	cruzar	to cross
		cruce	cross
de aquí	from here	el puente	bridge
en el centro de	in the middle of	la plaza	square
cerca de	near to	ir	to go
delante de	in front of	vaya	go
detrás de	behind	hasta	as far as
enfrente de	opposite	los semáforos	traffic lights
		pasar	to pass

pase	go past	torcer	to turn
todo derecho/todo recto	straight on	tuerza	turn
seguir	to keep	a la izquierda	left
siga todo recto	keep straight on	a la derecha	right
tomar/coger	to take	doblar la esquina	to turn the corner
tome/coja	take		
la primera calle	first street	doble la esquina	turn the corner
la segunda calle	second street	aquí	here
la tercera calle	third street	allí	there
la próxima calle	next street	allá	over there

◆ Foundation phrases

Perdone señora ¿dónde está el banco?	Excuse me madam, where is the bank?
¿Hay una farmacia por aquí?	Is there a chemists near here?
Por favor, señor ¿para ir al estadio?	Excuse me sir, how do I get to the stadium?
Siga todo derecho y está a la izquierda.	Keep straight on and it's on the left.
Tome la tercera calle a la derecha.	Take the third street on the right.
¿Está lejos? – No, está solamente a doscientos metros.	Is it far? – No, it is only two hundred metres away.

◆ Higher words

acercarse a	to approach	equivocarse de camino	to go the wrong way
alejarse de	to go away (from)		
la bocacalle	turning	girar	to turn
la carretera correcta	the right road	la glorieta	roundabout
dirigirse a	to make for	en la proximidad de	in the proximity of
errar el camino, extraviarse, perderse	to get lost		

◆ Higher phrases

¿Cuánto hay de aquí al río?	How far is it to the river?
Me he extraviado. ¿Puede usted ayudarme por favor?	I'm lost. Can you help me please?
¿Me puede indicar cómo llegar a la estación?	Can you direct me to the station?
¿A qué distancia queda?	How far away is it?
Justo a la vuelta de la esquina.	Just round the corner.

Shopping and Eating

SHOPS

◆ Foundation words

la tienda	shop	la librería	book shop
la carnicería	butcher's	el mercado	market
la confitería	sweet shop	la panadería	bakers
la droguería	hardware store	la pastelería	cake shop
electrodomésticos	electrical household appliances	la peluquería	hairdresser's
		la perfumería	perfume shop
		la pescadería	fish shop
el estanco	tobacconist	el quiosco (de periódicos)	news-stand
la farmacia	chemist	el supermercado	supermarket
la frutería	fruit shop	la tabacalera	tobacconist
los grandes almacenes	department store	la tienda de comestibles	grocers
		:de discos	record shop
la hamburguesería	burger bar	:de recuerdos	souvenir shop
el hipermercado	hypermarket	la zapatería	shoe shop

◆ Higher words

la charcutería	delicatessen	la joyería	jeweller
la churrería	fritter store	la limpieza en seco	dry cleaner's
la ferretería	hardware store	la relojería	watchmaker's
la floristería, florería	florist, florist's	la verdulería	greengrocer's

SHOPPING

◆ Foundation words

hacer (hago) la compra	to do (I do) the shopping	el/la cliente	customer
		comprar	to buy
ir (voy) de compras	to go (I go) shopping	¿cuánto?	how much
		¿cuánto cuesta (n)?	how much is it/are they?
		¿cuánto es/son?	
abrir	to open	¿cuánto vale (n)?	
abierto	open	dar	to give
cerrar	to close	deme	give me
cerrado	shut	el descuento	discount
¿algo más?	anything else?	desear	to want
el artículo	article	¿qué desea?	what can I get you?
la caja	till	¿eso es todo?	is that all?
cambiar	to change, exchange	gastar	to spend
		la liquidación	sale
el cambio	change	a mitad de precio	half price

necesitar	to need	la tarjeta de crédito	credit card
la oferta	offer	tener	to have
el precio	price	¿tiene…?	have you got any…?
querer (quiero)	to want (I want)		
quisiera…	I'd like…	vender	to sell
las rebajas	sales	el vendedor/la	shop assistant
grandes rebajas	big reductions	vendedora	
el recibo	receipt	'empujar'	push
rebajar	to reduce	'tirar'	pull
la rebaja	reduction	la planta baja	ground floor
la sección	department	el primer piso/	first floor
la sección de discos	record department	la primera planta	
		el segundo piso/	second floor
servir (sirvo)	to serve (I serve)	la segunda planta	
		el tercer piso/	third floor
¿en qué puedo servirle/servirla?	what can I get you?	la tercera planta	
		el cuarto piso/	fourth floor
el surtido	selection, range	la cuarta planta	

◆ **Foundation phrases**

¿A qué hora se abre?	What time does it open?
¿A qué hora se cierra?	What time does it shut?
Buenos días, ¿en qué puedo servirle/servirla?	Good day, what can I get you?
Deme una barra de pan por favor.	Give me a loaf of bread please.
Aquí tiene.	Here you are.
¿Algo más?	Anything else?
Sí, quisiera un melón.	Yes, I'd like a melon.
¿Qué le debo?	How much (is it)?
Me gusta ir de compras.	I like to go shopping.

◆ **Higher words**

el autoservicio	self service	envolver	to wrap up
el carrito	trolley	la escalera ambulante	escalator
la cesta	basket	el escaparate	shop window
comprar a plazos	to buy on hire purchase	ir a ver escaparates	to go window-shopping
curiosear	to browse	la ganga	bargain
devolver	to give back, repay	gratuito, gratis	free
		hacer falta	to need
entregar	to hand over, deliver	horas de apertura	opening hours
		el impuesto	tax
la entrega	delivery	el IVA	VAT
la entrega a domicilio	home delivery	la marca	brand, make

mostrar	to show	reembolsar	to reimburse
el mostrador	counter	el reembolso	refund
ofrecer	to offer	la selección	selection
el probador	changing room	el tendero/la tendera	shopkeeper
las provisiones	groceries	el valor	value
el puesto	stall	la venta	sale

◆ **Higher phrases**

Me gusta ir a ver escaparates con mis amigas.	I like to go window-shopping with my friends.
Quiero que me reembolse por favor.	I'd like my money back please.

Aceite de oliva
CARBONELL, 0,4°, L.
€1,40

Arroz
FALLERA, 2 kg.
€1,00

En abril, Ofertas Mil

REBAJAS FANTASTICAS

HIPERMERCADO
ALCAMPO
Fulminamos los precios.

¡OFERTA!

HORARIO:
De Lunes a Sábado
Mañanas de 9,30 a 1,30
—
Tardes de Lunes a Viernes
de 4 a 8,00

Día %
Autoservicio descuento.

F O O D   A N D   D R I N K

◆ **Foundation words**

la fruta	**fruit**	**las legumbres,**	**vegetables**
la aceituna	olive	**las verduras**	
la fresa	strawberry	el ajo	garlic
el limón	lemon	la cebolla	onion
la manzana	apple	los champiñones	mushrooms
el melocotón	peach	**la col**	cabbage
el melón	melon	la coliflor	cauliflower
la naranja	orange	los guisantes	peas
la pera	pear	**las judías verdes**	**green beans**
el plátano	banana	la lechuga	lettuce
el tomate	tomato	las patatas	potatoes
las uvas	grapes	**el pimiento**	**pepper**
		la zanahoria	carrot
un kilo de	a kilo of		
medio kilo de	half a kilo of		
doscientos gramos de	200 grammes of		

◆ **Foundation phrases**

Póngame un kilo de manzanas por favor.	I'll take a kilo of apples please.
¿Cuánto cuestan las patatas?	How much do the potatoes cost?

◆ Higher words

el albaricoque	apricot
la cereza	cherry
la ciruela	plum
la frambuesa	raspberry
la granada	pomegranate
el kiwi	kiwi fruit
el pomelo	grapefruit
la sandía	watermelon
las coles de Bruselas	Brussels sprouts
el espárrago	asparagus
la espinaca	spinach
los garbanzos	chick peas
las habas	broad beans
el pepino	cucumber

los comestibles	**groceries**
el agua mineral	mineral water
el arroz	rice
el azúcar	sugar
el café	coffee
los cereales	breakfast cereals
el croissán/croissant	croissant
los huevos	eggs
el jamón	ham
la leche	milk
la mantequilla	butter
la mermelada	jam

el pan	bread
la barra de pan	French stick, baguette
el panecillo	bread roll
el pastel	cake
las patatas fritas	crisps
la pimienta	pepper
el queso	cheese
la sal	salt
la salsa	sauce
la tarta	tart, cake
el té	tea
el vinagre	vinegar
el vino	wine
el yogur	yoghurt
el zumo de fruta	fruit juice
el bombón	chocolate (sweet)
el caramelo	sweet, candy
el chicle	chewing gum
el chocolate	chocolate (bar)
un bote de	jar of
una botella de	bottle of
una docena de	dozen
una lata de	tin of
un litro de	litre of
una loncha/lonja de	slice of
un paquete de	packet of
un pedazo de	piece of

◆ Foundation phrases

Quisiera una docena de huevos por favor.	I'd like a dozen eggs please.
También necesito un bote de mermelada.	I also need a jar of jam.

◆ Higher words

el aceite de oliva	olive oil
la almendra	almond
la harina	flour
el jugo de fruta	fruit juice
maduro	ripe

la miel	honey
la nuez	walnut
el turrón	nougat
una rebanada de (pan)	slice of (bread)

la tapa	**snack**
el bocadillo	sandwich
el churro	fritter
la hamburguesa	hamburger
las patatas fritas	chips, crisps
el perrito caliente	hot dog
la pizza	pizza
la porción de	small portion of
la ración de	large portion of
los entremeses	**starters**
la ensalada	salad
la ensalada mixta	mixed salad
el gazpacho	cold vegetable soup
la sopa	soup
la carne	**meat**
el bistec	steak
el cordero	lamb
la carne de cerdo	pork
la carne de vaca	beef
el chorizo	dry pork sausage
la chuleta	chop
el filete	steak
el jamón	ham
:de York	boiled ham
:serrano	cured ham
el pollo	chicken
la salchicha	sausage
el salchichón	(salami-type) sausage
asar	to roast
asado	roast
freír	to fry
frito	fried
vegetariano	vegetarian
el pescado	**fish**
el atún	tuna
el bacalao	cod
la merluza	hake
el salmón	salmon

las sardinas	sardines
los mariscos	shell fish
los calamares	squid
las gambas	prawns
los huevos	**eggs**
la tortilla	omelette
la tortilla española	Spanish omelette
el arroz	rice
la paella	paella
la pasta	pasta
el postre	**sweet, dessert**
el flan	caramel cream
el helado	ice-cream
:de chocolate	chocolate ice-cream
:de fresa	strawberry ice-cream
:de vainilla	vanilla ice-cream
la nata	cream
el pastel	cake
el queso	cheese
la tarta	cake, tart
el yogur	yoghurt
apetitoso	appetizing
rico	delicious, tasty
oler (huele) a	to smell (it smells) of
el olor	smell
saber a	to taste of
el sabor	taste
la bebida	**drink**
el agua	water
el agua mineral	mineral water
:con gas	fizzy mineral water
:sin gas	flat mineral water
el café	coffee
:con leche	white coffee
:solo	black coffee

la cerveza	beer	la sangría	sangria (red wine with fruit)
el champán	champagne	el té	tea
el chocolate	chocolate	el vino	wine
la cocacola	coca cola	:blanco	white wine
la gaseosa	pop, fizzy drink	:tinto	red wine
el jugo de fruta	fruit juice	el zumo de fruta	fruit juice
la leche	milk	una taza (de)	a cup (of)
la limonada	lemonade	un vaso (de)	a glass (of)
la naranjada	orange squash		
el refresco	cool drink		

◆ **Foundation phrases**

Mi comida favorita es el pollo.	My favourite food is chicken.
Me gustan mucho las hamburguesas.	I like hamburgers a lot.
Me encanta el arroz.	I love rice.
Detesto las aceitunas.	I hate olives.
Lo siento pero no me gusta.	I'm sorry but I don't like it.
Para el desayuno tomo café con leche y tostada.	At breakfast I have white coffee and toast.
Soy vegetariano.	I'm a vegetarian.
La paella es un plato típico español.	Paella is a typical Spanish dish.

◆ **Higher words**

el pincho	snack	la ostra	oyster
un pincho de tortilla	a portion of omelette	el pulpo	octopus
		la trucha	trout
el caracol	snail		
el cocido	stew	el crepe	pancake
el ganso	goose	el pastel	cake, tart
el pato	duck		
el pavo	turkey	picante	hot, spicy
rellenar	to stuff	sabroso	tasty
el relleno	stuffing	salado	salty
el solomillo	sirloin	saborear	to taste, flavour
la ternera	veal		
bien hecho, muy hecho	well done	el batido	milk shake
poco hecho	rare	el coñac	brandy
a la parrilla, a la plancha	grilled	el cortado	coffee with a little milk
los boquerones	anchovies	la ginebra	gin
el cangrejo	crab	el jerez	sherry
la langosta	lobster	la sidra	cider
los mejillones	mussels	el vino rosado	rosé wine

◆ **Higher phrases**

Quisiera mi filete bien hecho.	I'd like my steak well done.
Esta paella está riquísima.	This paella is really tasty.
¿Has probado el pulpo?	Have you tried octopus?

¡BUEN PROVECHO!

PIZZA-PIZZA

servicio gratuito a domicilio.
Pizzas recién hechas.
En tu casa, en menos de 30 minutos

— M E N U —

MARGARITA	Queso y tomate.
VEGETAL	Queso, tomate, champiñones, pimiento verde, aceitunas y cebolla.
HAWAIANA	Piña y jámon.
PIAMONTESA	Salami, bacon, champiñones.
PICANTE	Carne, guindilla y salsa picante.
RODEO	Carne, bacon y salsa barbacoa.
BOLOGNESA	Queso, tomate, carne y cebolla.
ATLANTICA	Atún, cebolla, aceitunas verdes, queso y tomate.

Comidas

Sopa	€0,75
Ensalada	€0,90
Sardinas	€1,20
Pimientos de padrón	€1,00
Calamares a la romana	€3,00
Gambas a la plancha	€3,00
Merluza a la romana	€2,80
Ternera asada	€3,00
Chuletas de ternera	€3,60
Chuletas de cerdo	€2,20

DESAYUNOS
PLATOS COMBINADOS
SANDWICHES
BOCADILLOS
POSTRES VARIADOS

CAFÉS AND RESTAURANTS

◆ Foundation words

el café, la cafetería	café	¿qué es...?	what is...?
el restaurante	restaurant	recomendar	to recommend
reservar	to reserve	¿qué recomienda?	what do you recommend?
la mesa	table		
para	for		
una persona	one	la cuchara	spoon
dos personas	two people	el cuchillo	knife
el camarero	waiter	el mantel	table cloth
la camarera	waitress	el platillo	saucer
¡camarero!	(used to call the waiter) waiter!	el plato	plate
		la servilleta	serviette
¡señorita!	(used to call the waitress) waitress!	la taza	cup
		el tenedor	fork
la carta	à la carte menu	el vaso	glass
el menú	menu	faltar	to be missing
el menú del día	fixed price meal	sucio	dirty
el plato del día	dish of the day		
el plato principal	main course	¡salud!	cheers!
para empezar	to start	¡qué aproveche!	enjoy your meal!
para beber	to drink		
el aperitivo	aperitif	la cuenta	bill
¡oiga!	hey! (to waiter/ waitress)	el error	mistake
		incluido	included
traer	to bring	pagar	to pay
tráigame... por favor	bring me... please	la propina	tip
		el servicio	service charge

◆ Foundation phrases

Somos cinco.	There are five of us.
Quisiera una mesa para dos personas.	I'd like a table for two.
Tengo una mesa reservada en la terraza.	I have a table reserved on the terrace.
Falta un tenedor.	There's a fork missing.
¿Dónde está el teléfono?	Where's the phone?
¿Dónde están los servicios?	Where are the toilets?
Deme una cocacola por favor.	Give me a cola, please.
Quiero el menú de ocho euros.	I'd like the eight euros menu.
¿Me puede decir qué es el cocido?	Can you tell me what "cocido" is?
Para empezar voy a tomar sopa.	I'll have soup to start.
Hay un error.	There is a mistake.

◆ **Higher words**

el alimento, la alimentación	food	medio hecho	medium done
el ambiente	atmosphere	el menú turístico	tourist menu
apetecer	to fancy	oler a	to smell of
me apetece	I fancy	huele a	it smells of
la bandeja	tray	los platos combinados	set main course
el cenicero	ashtray	quedar satisfecho	to be full
componerse de	to consist of	la receta	recipe
decepcionado	disappointed	sazonar (de)	to season (with)
estar decepcionado con	to be disappointed with	agitar	to stir
la especialidad	speciality	añadir	to add
guisar	to cook	batir	to beat
el jefe/la jefa de cocina	chef	cortar	to cut
		mezclar	to mix
		pelar	to peel

◆ **Higher phrases**

No puedo más.	I'm full up.
Quiero quejarme. La sopa está fría.	I want to complain. The soup is cold.
La camarera fue muy simpática/antipática.	The waitress was very nice/rude.
¡Quédese con la vuelta!	Keep the change!
Me han cobrado de más.	I've been overcharged.

El Olivio Bar
tu música • tu marcha • tu ambiente

Alubias Verdes
Sopa de Cocido
Garbanzos
San Jacobos
lenguado
Postre: Flan, Tarta de manzana
(Bebida no incluida)
Precio €6

CLOTHES AND JEWELLERY

◆ Foundation words

el abrigo	overcoat	la talla	size (clothes)
el bañador	trunks, swimsuit	el número	size (shoes)
		muy	very
la blusa	blouse	demasiado	too
las botas	boots	grande	big
los calcetines	socks	pequeño	small
la camiseta	tee shirt	mediano	medium
el chandal	track suit	corto	short
el cinturón	belt	largo	long
la corbata	tie	barato	cheap
la falda	skirt	caro	dear
los guantes	gloves	elegante	smart
el impermeable	raincoat		
el jersey	jumper, jersey	el algodón	cotton
las medias	tights, stockings	el cuero	leather
el pantalón	trousers	la lana	wool
el pantalón corto	shorts	el plástico	plastic
el panty/los pantis	tights	la seda	silk
el pijama	pyjamas		
las sandalias	sandals	los pendientes	earrings
el sombrero	hat	el reloj	watch
el suéter	sweater	el diamante	diamond
el traje	suit	el oro	gold
el traje de baño	swimming costume	la plata	silver
los vaqueros	jeans		
el vestido	dress		
las zapatillas deportivas/ de deporte	trainers		
los zapatos	shoes		
probarse	to try on		

rompecabezas:	riddle:
oro no es	it's not gold
plata no es	it's not silver
¿qué es?	what is it?
Answer on page 109	

◆ Foundation phrases

Quisiera comprar un jersey azul.	I want to buy a blue jumper.
Lo siento, no quedan.	I'm sorry, there are none left.
Me gusta mucho este pantalón.	I like these trousers a lot.
Es demasiado grande.	It is too big.
¿Tiene otro en verde?	Have you got another in green?
¿Puedo probármelo?	Can I try it on?
¿No tiene algo más barato?	Haven't you got anything cheaper?
Te queda/sienta bien.	It suits you.

◆ Higher words

la americana	sports jacket	la ropa interior	underwear
la bata	dressing gown	el sostén	bra
el bikini	bikini	los tejanos	jeans
las bragas	knickers, panties		
la bufanda	scarf	la manga	sleeve
calzar	to wear, take (shoe)	con manga corta	short sleeved
los calzoncillos	underpants	con manga larga	long sleeved
el calzón	boxer shorts	de moda	fashionable
la camisa	shirt	la cremallera	zip
la cazadora	(bomber) jacket	la percha	coat-hanger
el chaleco	waistcoat		
la chaqueta	jacket	la joya	jewel
la chaqueta de cuero	leather jacket	el anillo	ring
el conjunto	outfit	el broche	brooch
a cuadros	check	la cadena	chain
el gorro/la gorra	cap	el collar	necklace
la rebeca	cardigan	la pulsera	bracelet
		la sortija	ring

◆ Higher phrases

Ese conjunto te sienta bien.	You look nice in that outfit.
No sé qué ponerme.	I don't know what to wear.
¿Qué número calza usted?	What size shoe do you take?
Para la boda llevaba un sombrero azul.	She wore a blue hat for the wedding.
Me sienta perfectamente.	It fits me perfectly.

◆ Sopa de letras

Find the words in the wordsearch.

SOMBRERO
CAMISA
BLUSA
FALDA
CORBATA
BOTAS
ZAPATO
CAMISETA
CHAQUETA
PANTALON
VESTIDO
ABRIGO
VAQUEROS
JERSEY

(Answer on page 109)

S	A	G	I	N	O	L	A	C	N	A	A
O	C	Z	C	A	M	F	R	O	C	T	P
S	A	A	A	H	A	O	L	B	E	A	A
O	M	P	M	L	A	A	L	U	N	B	B
R	O	A	D	I	T	U	Q	O	O	V	R
E	G	A	E	N	S	A	R	T	E	E	I
U	I	C	A	A	H	E	A	S	O	S	J
Q	R	P	S	C	R	S	T	T	R	E	J
A	B	N	I	B	D	I	A	A	R	O	C
V	A	T	M	L	D	P	E	S	R	E	J
Q	O	O	A	O	A	Y	E	S	R	E	J
B	S	F	C	Z	A	T	A	B	R	O	C

SOUVENIRS AND TOILETRIES

◆ Foundation words

el recuerdo	souvenirs	el cepillo	brush
el regalo	present	el cepillo de dientes	tooth brush
el abanico	fan	el champú	shampoo
las castañuelas	castanets	el desodorante	deodorant
las cerillas	matches	el jabón	soap
la cerámica	pottery	la pasta de dientes	tooth
el llavero	key-ring	el peine	comb
la muñeca	doll	el perfume	perfume

◆ Higher words

el cigarro	cigar	la barra de labios	lipstick
el encendedor,	cigarette lighter	la compresa	sanitary towel
el mechero		la crema bronceadora	suntan cream
la pintura	painting	el esmalte	nail varnish
la pipa	pipe	el pañuelo de papel	paper
el monedero,	purse		handkerchief
el portamonedas		el tampón	tampon

Transport

◆ **Foundation words**

el transporte (público)	(public) transport	llegar	to arrive
el vehículo	**vehicle**	**ponerse (me pongo)** en camino	**to set off (I set off)**
el autobús	bus	salir	to leave
en autobús	by bus	venir (vengo)	to come (I come)
el autocar	coach	viajar	to travel
el avión	plane	el viajero	traveller
el barco	boat	el viaje	journey
la bicicleta (bici)	bike	¡buen viaje!	have a good journey!
:de montaña	**mountain bike**		
el coche	car	**durar**	**to last**
el ferry (ferri)	**ferry**	visitar	to visit
el metro	underground, tube	la visita	visit
		coger	to catch
la moto	motorbike	**perder**	**to miss**
a pie	on foot	¿hay?	is there?
el tranvía	**tram**	el asiento	seat
el tren	train	libre	free
		ocupado	occupied
andar, ir a pie	to walk	el conductor	driver
ir (voy)	to go (1 go)	**el pasajero**	**passenger**

◆ **Foundation phrases**

¿Cuándo quiere usted viajar?	When do you want to travel?
Quisiera ir a Madrid el sábado.	I'd like to go to Madrid on Saturday.
Normalmente voy al colegio en autobús.	I normally go to school by bus.
¿Cuánto tiempo dura el viaje?	How long does the journey last?
Dura diez minutos.	It lasts 10 minutes.

◆ **Higher words**

apresurarse, darse prisa	to hurry	la etapa	stage
dar una vuelta	to go for a stroll	marcharse	to go (away), leave
el retraso	delay		
retrasar(se)	to delay	recorrer	to travel through
de prisa	quickly		
desplazar	to travel, go (so far)	el recorrido	journey, route
		el trayecto	way, journey

◆ **Higher phrases**

Vinimos andando.	We came on foot.
¿Qué tal el viaje?	What was the journey like?
Fue muy aburrido y cansado.	It was very boring and tiring.

CARS AND BIKES

◆ Foundation words

acceso prohibido	no entry	la dirección obligatoria, única	one way
el aceite	oil	la gasolina	petrol
el aparcamiento	car park	:sin plomo	unleaded petrol
aparcar	to park	la súper	four star petrol
la autopista	motorway	el motor	engine
el carnet de conducir	driving licence	el paso de peatones	pedestrian crossing
la carretera	main road		
la circulación	traffic	el radiador	radiator
conducir	to drive	el semáforo	traffic lights
el conductor	motorist, driver		
la dirección	direction		

◆ Higher words

acelerar	to accelerate	la matrícula	number plate
la acera	pavement	moderar la velocidad	to reduce speed
adelantar	to overtake	la marcha atrás	reverse gear
arrancar	to start	la multa	fine
el atasco	traffic jam	poner una multa	to give a fine
atropellar	to knock down	las obras	road works
la auto-escuela	driving school	el parabrisas	windscreen
la avería	breakdown	el peaje	toll
averiarse	to break down	la periférica	ring road
la baca	roof rack	el permiso de conducir	driving licence
la batería	battery	pinchado	flat (tyre)
la carretera periférica de circunvalación	ring road	el pinchazo	puncture
		la presión	pressure
el casco	helmet	¡prohibido el paso!	no entry!
¡ceda el paso!	give way!	la red de autopistas	motorway network
chocar con/contra	to bump into		
la curva	bend	el retrovisor	rear view mirror
desviar	to divert		
el desvío	detour	revisar	to check
el diesel	diesel oil	la rueda	wheel
el estacionamiento	parking	la señal	sign post
estacionar	to park	el sentido único	one way
el faro	headlamp	el vehículo todo terreno	4-wheel-drive vehicle
frenar	to brake		
el freno	brake	la velocidad máxima	speed limit
la glorieta	roundabout	la ventanilla	car window
la hora punta	rush hour	verificar	to check
el maletero	boot	el volante	steering wheel

◆ Higher phrases

Tengo un pinchazo.	I've got a puncture.
Mi coche está averiado en la M30.	My car has broken down on the M30.
Podría enviar al mecánico por favor.	Could you send me a mechanic please.
Ha habido un accidente.	There has been an accident.
Puede revisar el aceite por favor.	Could you please check the oil.

NO APARCAR

SALIDA DE EMERGENCIA

CEDA EL PASO

PELIGRO

OBRAS

EN 7 Km.

120 min.
EXCEPTO
RESIDENTES

Laborales: 10.00 a 14.00 horas
y : 16.00 a 20.00 horas
Sábados : 10.00 a 14.00 horas

AREA
DE APARCAMIENTO
REGULADO Y CONTROLADO

BUSES AND TRAINS

◆ Foundation words

coger	to catch	de primera/segunda	first/second
el autobús	bus	clase	class
el bonobús	bus pass, book of bus tickets	(no) fumador	(non)-smoker
el cobrador	conductor	el andén	platform
la estación de autobuses	bus station	la consigna	left luggage office
		el horario	timetable
la estación (de ferrocarril)	train station	el paso subterráneo	subway
		la sala de espera	waiting room
la parada	bus stop	la salida	exit
bajar de	to get off	la vía	track
subir a	to get on	RENFE	Spanish rail network
la llegada	arrival		
la salida	departure	el expreso, el rápido	express train
el anuncio	announcement	el AVE, el Talgo	high speed trains
el despacho de billetes, la taquilla	ticket office	con destino a	to
sacar un billete	to get a ticket	procedente de	from
		el retraso	delay
el billete	ticket	el revisor	ticket collector
:de ida, sencillo	single	el suplemento	excess fare
:de ida y vuelta	return	el transbordo	change

◆ Foundation phrases

¿A qué hora sale el tren?	What time does the train leave?
¿De qué andén?	From which platform?
¿Es éste el autobús para Segovia?	Is this the bus to Segovia?
¿Dónde está la parada?	Where is the bus stop?
Es el autobús número quince.	It's bus number fifteen.
Quiero un billete de ida y vuelta.	I want a return ticket.
El tren llega con veinte minutos de retraso.	The train is twenty minutes late.

◆ Higher words

atrasar	to delay	el paso a nivel	level crossing
el coche cama	sleeping car	el portaequipajes	luggage rack
el coche comedor, restaurante	restaurant car	con destino	heading for
el compartimiento	compartment	transbordar	to change
		hacer transbordo en	to change at

◆ **Higher phrases**

¡Señores viajeros al tren!	Will passengers kindly board the train!
El tren procedente de Barcelona llegará dentro de poco.	The train from Barcelona will arrive shortly.
Lo siento, me olvidé de comprar un billete.	I'm sorry, I forgot to buy a ticket.

*INFORMACION
RENFE

733 22 00
733 30 00

DESCUENTOS APLICABLES
EN LOS DIAS AZULES DE RENFE

TARJETA FAMILIAR: 50% a 75%.
TARJETA DORADA: 50%.
IDA Y VUELTA: 20%.
GRUPOS: 20% a 30%.
DEPARTAMENTO EXCLUSIVO
OFERTA "8 x 5" y "6 x 4"
VIAJE CON SU PAREJA EN
COCHE-CAMA.
TARJETA JOVEN: 50% Y UN
RECORRIDO GRATIS EN LITERA
(Mayo a Diciembre).
AUTO-EXPRESO: 20% a 100%.
LOS DESCUENTOS SON SOBRE
"TARIFA GENERAL", EXCLUIDOS
LOS SUPLEMENTOS

INSTRUCCIONES

* Esta tarjeta se utilizará únicamente en las lineas normales de autobuses. Será válida como título de transporte hasta el próximo cambio de tarifas.
* Por favor, no doble la tarjeta.
* En caso de cualquier anomalía, presente la tarjeta al cobrador del autobus.
* La tarjeta será presentada a cualquier empleado de la empresa que lo solicite.
* Este documento podrá ser retirado en caso de uso indebido.
* 7% I.V.A. Incluido.
* S.O.V. Incluido.
* C.I.F.A-28046316

BONO
BUENO
EL
BONO BUS
* **rapidez**
* **comodidad**
* **economia**

BOATS AND PLANES

◆ Foundation words

el aeropuerto	airport	volar	to fly
el piloto/la pilota	pilot	el puerto	port
el vuelo	flight		

◆ Foundation phrases

¿A qué hora sale el vuelo a Londres? — What time does the flight to London leave?

¿Hay una cafetería en el aeropuerto? — Is there a cafe in the airport?

◆ Higher words

abrochar	to fasten (safety belt)	desembarcar	to disembark
aterrizar	to land	embarcar	to embark
el aterrizaje	landing	el embarcadero	jetty, pier
la azafata	air hostess	la lancha a motor	motor boat
despegar	to take off	la marea alta	high tide
la nave espacial	spaceship	la marea baja	low tide
el bote, el barco	boat	la travesía	crossing
el bote a remo	rowing boat	volcar	to capsize, overturn

◆ Higher phrases

Por poco pierdo el vuelo. — I almost missed the flight.

El aterrizaje fue horroroso. — The landing was terrifying.

Abrochense los cinturones de seguridad por favor. — Fasten your seat belts please.

◆ **Rompecabezas**

Fill in the puzzle with the Spanish words for these forms of transport:

1. taxi
2. boat
3. bus
4. plane
5. motorbike
6. bicycle
7. foot
8. train

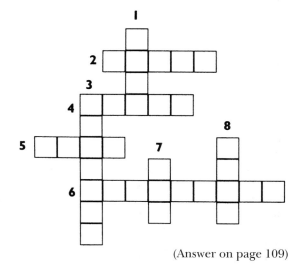

(Answer on page 109)

General

◆ **Colours**

los colores	colours
blanco	white
negro	black
gris	grey
rojo	red
amarillo	yellow
verde	green
azul	blue
marrón	chestnut, brown
rosa	pink
violeta	violet
purpúreo	purple
naranja	orange
crema	cream
oscuro	dark
claro	light

◆ **Days**

lunes	Monday
martes	Tuesday
miércoles	Wednesday
jueves	Thursday
viernes	Friday
sábado	Saturday
domingo	Sunday

◆ **Months**

enero	January
febrero	February
marzo	March
abril	April
mayo	May
junio	June
julio	July
agosto	August
setiembre	September
octubre	October
noviembre	November
diciembre	December

◆ **Seasons**

la primavera	spring
el verano	summer
el otoño	autumn
el invierno	winter

◆ **Dates**

la fecha	date
¿a cuántos estamos?	what's the date?
¿qué fecha es?	what's the date?
estamos a seis de mayo	it's May 6
es el seis de mayo	it's May 6
desde	from
hasta	till
a partir de	from

◆ **Time Expressions**

el segundo	second
el minuto	minute
la hora	hour
el día	day
la semana	week
ocho días	week
dos semanas	fortnight
quince días	fortnight
el mes	month
el año	year
el siglo	century
la mañana	morning
la tarde	afternoon
la noche	night
por la mañana	in the morning
por la tarde	in the afternoon
por la noche	at night
hoy	today
esta noche	tonight
ayer	yesterday
anoche	last night
mañana	tomorrow
mañana por la mañana	tomorrow morning

pasado mañana	the day after tomorrow
el lunes	on Monday
los sábados	on Saturdays
el lunes próximo	next Monday
el lunes pasado	last Monday
esta semana	this week
el fin de semana	(at the) weekend
ahora	now
inmediatamente	immediately
enseguida	straight away
ahora mismo	right now
entonces	then
luego	next
antes (de)	before
después (de)	after
durante	during
temprano	early
tarde	late
pronto	soon
hace dos días	two days ago

◆ Clock

¿qué hora es?	what time is it?
es la una	it's one o'clock
son las dos	it's two o'clock
a las dos	at two o'clock
y cuarto	quarter past
y media	half past
menos cuarto	quarter to
mediodía	noon
medianoche	midnight
de la mañana	a.m.
de la tarde/noche	p.m.
a eso de	about
en punto	exactly, on the dot

◆ Frequency

generalmente	generally
normalmente	normally, usually
a veces	sometimes
muchas veces	often
siempre	always

pocas veces	seldom
rara vez	rarely
nunca	never
todos los días	every day
todos los sábados	every Saturday
una vez	once
dos veces	twice
por día/al día	a day
dos veces por/a la semana	twice a week
otra vez	again
de nuevo	again

◆ Adjectives

muy	very
bastante	quite
fenomenal	great
estupendo	great
fantástico	fantastic
maravilloso	marvellous
agradable	pleasant
bonito	nice
perfecto	perfect
ideal	ideal
excelente	excellent
especial	special
bueno	good
interesante	interesting
horrible	horrible
terrible	terrible
feo	ugly, nasty
fatal	awful
desagradable	unpleasant
malo	bad
aburrido	boring
mejor	better
peor	worse
igual, mismo	same
parecido	similar
limpio	clean
sucio	dirty
barato	cheap

GENERAL

caro	expensive
fácil	easy
difícil	difficult
duro	hard
sencillo	simple
práctico	practical
útil	useful
importante	important
justo	fair, just
injusto	unfair, unjust
divertido	enjoyable, funny
emocionante	exciting
tranquilo	peaceful, quiet
ruidoso	noisy
típico	typical
rápido	quick, fast
lento	slow

◆ Linking words

y	and
o	or
con	with
sin	without
pero	but
si	if
entonces	then
luego	next, later
cuando	when
donde	where
por eso	so
porque	because
afortunadamente	fortunately
desafortunadamente	unfortunately
sin embargo	however
rápidamente	quickly
de repente	suddenly

◆ Opinions

sí	yes
no	no
en mi opinión	in my opinion
creo que	I think that
¿qué te parece?	what do you think?
estoy a favor (de)	I'm in favour (of)

es verdad	it's true
es falso	that's not right
tener razón	to be right
no tener razón	to be wrong
estar en contra (de)	to be against
estar equivocado	to be mistaken
gustar	to like
me gusta	I like
no me gusta	I don't like
encantar	to love
me encanta	I love
detestar, odiar	to hate
preferir (prefiero)	to prefer (I prefer)
estar de acuerdo	to agree
¿estás de acuerdo?	do you agree?
sí, estoy de acuerdo	yes, I agree
de acuerdo	agreed
vale	OK

◆ Position words

cerca de	near to
lejos de	far from
al lado de	next to
delante de	in front of
detrás de	behind
enfrente de	opposite
debajo de	under
encima de	above, on top of
en	in, at, on
sobre	on
en el centro de	in the middle of
al fondo de	at the back of
entre	between
hasta	as far as, until
a la izquierda	on the left
a la derecha	on the right
dentro de	inside, within
fuera de	outside
arriba	up, upstairs
abajo	down, downstairs
aquí	here
allí	there
por todas partes	everywhere

◆ Higher words

anteayer	day before yesterday
la víspera	evening before
el día anterior	day before
a primeros de, a principios de	at the beginning of
a mediados de	in the middle of
a finales de, a últimos de	at the end of
una quincena	a fortnight
adelantar, estar adelantado	to be fast (time)
estar atrasado, atrasar	to be slow (time)
de la madrugada	in the very early hours

◆ Numbers 1–19

cero	zero
uno	one
dos	two
tres	three
cuatro	four
cinco	five
seis	six
siete	seven
ocho	eight
nueve	nine
diez	ten
once	eleven
doce	twelve
trece	thirteen

catorce	fourteen
quince	fifteen
dieciséis	sixteen
diecisiete	seventeen
dieciocho	eighteen
diecinueve	nineteen

◆ Numbers 20–1,000,000

veinte	twenty
veintiuno	twenty one
veintidós	twenty two
veintitrés	twenty three
veinticuatro	twenty four
treinta	thirty
treinta y tres	thirty three
cuarenta	forty
cincuenta	fifty
sesenta	sixty
setenta	seventy
ochenta	eighty
noventa	ninety
ciento (cien)	one hundred (before noun)
ciento cincuenta	one hundred and fifty
doscientos	two hundred
trescientos	three hundred
quinientos	five hundred
setecientos	seven hundred
novecientos	nine hundred
mil	one thousand
un millón	one million

Building up Vocabulary

It is surprising how quickly you can build up vocabulary.
Try to make learning an enjoyable process:

- set yourself realistic targets
- get a friend to test you
- make learning cards
- use a computer
- if you like drawing, do some illustrations

The following pages have suggestions to help you increase your vocabulary.

 A lot of words are the same in Spanish as they are in English:

Examples: el hotel   el hospital   el animal   el póster   el hámster

Many words in Spanish are very similar to their English equivalent. The following examples should help you to work out their meaning.

 Sometimes the Spanish word simply adds another letter to the English:

Examples: el plano   el monumento   la visita   la lista   el uniforme   el restaurante

 Spanish words ending in "sión" are often the same, or nearly the same, as English words ending in "sion":

Examples: excursión (excursion)   decisión (decision)   discusión (discussion)

 Words ending in "tion" in English are often changed to "ción" in Spanish:

Examples: nación (nation)   información (information)   estación (station)

 "ph" in English is replaced in Spanish by the letter "f":

Examples: elefante (elephant)   foto (photo)   farmacia (pharmacy)   física (physics)

 Words ending in "y" in English often change to "ía" or "ia" in Spanish:

Examples: biología (biology)   tecnología (technology)   categoría (category)

7 **The ending "ty" in English often becomes "dad" in Spanish:**

Examples: la ciudad (city)　la electricidad (electricity)　la calidad (quality)

 8 **"ic(al)" in English is often translated by "ico" in Spanish:**

Examples: eléctrico (electric(al))　práctico (practical)　físico (physical)

 9 **"th" in English often becomes simply "t" in Spanish:**

Examples: catedral (cathedral)　teatro (theatre)　simpatía (sympathy)

 10 **Words ending in "ant" or "ent" in English often become "ante" or "ente" in Spanish:**

Examples: protestante (protestant)　incompetente (incompetent)　elefante (elephant)

 11 **Adverbs ending in "ly" end in "mente" in Spanish:**

Examples: normalmente (normally)　generalmente (generally)

 12 **The prefix "un" usually becomes "in" in Spanish:**

Examples: incompleto (unfinished)　injusto (unfair)　insoportable (unbearable)

 13 **Verbs in Spanish are very often based upon a noun:**

Examples: la cena/cenar (supper/to have supper)　el juego/jugar (game/to play)

 14 **Some adjectives (describing words) are often similar to the noun:**

Examples: la religión/religioso (religion/religious)　el ruido/ruidoso (noise/noisy)

15 **The Spanish endings "ito/a" and "illo/a" are used to make something smaller:**

Examples: la casa/la casita (house/small house)　el perro/el perrito (dog/puppy)

 16 **The Spanish ending "ón/ona" is used to make something bigger:**

Example: el hombre/el hombrón (man/big man)

BUILDING UP VOCABULARY

 If you come across a word you have never seen before, try to guess its meaning by looking for clues. Ask yourself:

● Is it like the English?

Examples:

el estómago	stomach
la ambulancia	ambulance

● Can you see part of a word you already know within the word?

Examples:

insolación
you know the word "sol" means "sun" and, from the rest of the sentence, you may
work out that "insolación" means "sunstroke"
acercarse
you know the word "cerca" means "near" – this is a verb which means
"to come near", "to approach"

● Is the word similar to a word you may have learned in French?

Examples:

iglesia	(like église)	church
piscina	(like piscine)	swimming pool
grande	(like grand)	big

● Is the word made up of two parts?

Examples:

el lavaplatos	dishwasher
el sacacorchos	corkscrew
el abrelatas	tin opener

Words to Watch Out For

 Sometimes words can be confusing if there is only one letter different:

Examples:

hoy	today	el bote	can, boat
hay	there is/are	la bota	boot
el hombre	man	pero	but
el hambre	hunger	el perro	dog
el puerto	port	lleno	full
la puerta	door	llano	flat
el cuarto	room	llegar	to arrive
cuatro	four	llevar	to wear, carry
		llenar	to fill
¿cuándo?	when?		
¿cuánto?	how much?	libre	free
		la libra	pound
el jamón	ham		
el jabón	soap	el plato	plate
		la plata	silver
casado	married		
cansado	tired	gastar	to spend
		ganar	to earn, win
la playa	beach	gustar	to like
la plaza	square		
caro	expensive		
la cara	face		

 Sometimes the accent makes all the difference:

Examples:

si	if
sí	yes
sólo	only
solo	alone

WORDS TO WATCH OUT FOR

 Sometimes the way the letters are arranged can lead to confusion:

Examples:

el camino	road
el camión	lorry
la película	film
la peluquería	hairdressers
la ciudad	city
cuidado	be careful

 Amigos falsos (false friends). Sometimes a Spanish word looks like a word in English, but means something completely different:

Examples:

el pan	bread	suspender	to fail (exam)
la ropa	clothes	asistir	to attend
largo	long	el conductor	driver
el motor	engine	los parientes	relatives
el músico	musician	la mermelada	jam
el fotógrafo	photographer	la planta baja	ground floor
embarazada	pregnant	el gato	cat
la librería	bookshop	mayor	elder, main
el wáter	toilet	la sopa	soup
el pie	foot	estar constipado	to have a cold
el éxito	success		

 Sometimes a word has more than one meaning in Spanish:

Examples:

la muñeca	wrist	doll
la tienda	shop	tent
la piel	skin	leather
llevar	to wear	to carry
la fiesta	festival	party
el campo	field	country

Writing Tips

FOUNDATION LEVEL

For the foundation writing paper at GCSE you will be asked to write a list or message and a letter, which is usually of an informal nature to a friend, but which could be of a formal nature to a hotel, campsite, etc. Here are some tips for you:

- Keep your writing simple. Use words and phrases in Spanish that you have used before and which you feel confident about.

- NEVER write out your answer in English before trying to translate it into Spanish – that can lead to all sorts of mistakes.

- MAKE SURE YOU COVER ALL THE POINTS YOU ARE ASKED TO. This is most important because, if you don't, you will lose marks on content. Put a tick next to each task on the question paper once you have answered it.

- Sometimes you can get clues from the letter on the question paper – it is simply a question of re-using some of the words and phrases for your own purposes. Remember in your reply that you are talking about yourself, so in the present tense you need to change regular verb endings to "o":

  Examples:
¿Por qué quieres este empleo?	Why do you want this job?
Quiero este empleo porque…	I want this job because…
¿Adónde vas de vacaciones?	Where are you going on holiday?
Voy a España.	I'm going to Spain.

- In the letter you will also have to ask some questions. If it is a letter to a friend, remember that the verb will probably end in "s":

  Examples:
¿Adónde vas?	Where are you going?
¿Tienes…?	Have you got…?
¿Prefieres…?	Do you prefer…?

  But
¿Te gusta el colegio?	Do you like school?
¿Te gustan los deportes?	Do you like sports?

- If the letter is formal and you are asking questions, remember to remove the "s" from the end of the verb.

  Example:
¿Puede reservarme…?	Can you reserve me…?

WRITING TIPS

- Here are some useful questions for letters:

¿Qué tiempo hace...?	What is the weather like...?
¿Hay...?	Is/are there...?
¿A qué hora...?	What time...?
¿Cómo es...?	What is... like?
¿Cuál es/qué es...?	What is...?

But

¿Cómo se llama...?	What is... called?
¿Cómo se llama tu hermano?	What is your brother called?
¿Por qué...?	Why...?
¿Cuánto tiempo...?	How long...?

- Remember to put your town and date on the right of your letter.

  Example:
  Durham, 21 de mayo

- Make sure you have the correct beginning for your letter.

  Examples:

Querido	(to a male friend)
Querida	(to a female friend)
Muy señor mío	(to a male stranger)
Muy señora mía	(to a female stranger)

- Make sure you have the correct ending for your letter.

  Examples:

un abrazo de	(to a friend)
hasta pronto	(to a friend)
con el afectuoso saludo	(to a friend)
le saluda atentamente	(to a stranger)

- Take care in your work. Try to be neat and accurate. Avoid crossing out. If you have time, do a rough version, then copy it up. If one sentence is causing you problems, write it out in rough on the supplementary paper provided.

- Check for:
  a) Spellings – remember that the only double consonants in Spanish are "ll" "cc" "rr" "nn"
  b) Agreement of describing words – "la ciudad bonit<u>a</u>"
  c) Position of describing words – in Spanish, most come after the noun: "la falda <u>azul</u>"
  d) Verbs – make sure that it is the right verb and that you have: the right tense, the right person and the right ending
  e) "a" followed by "el" changing to "al" – "fui <u>al</u> pueblo"
  f) "de" followed by "el" changing to "del" – "saqué la foto <u>del</u> monumento"

- Try to use separate paragraphs for the different points you are making. This is quite easy if you look back to the letter on the question paper.

- Don't be afraid to show off a bit to the examiner if there are things you have learned which you feel you can bring into your reply. The examiner will be impressed by such things as:
  a) al" "antes de" "después de" "para," "sin" + infinitive
  b) Opinions – "me gusta" etc. Reasons – "porque es interesante"
  c) Linking words – "cuando" "donde" "que"
  d) Expressions using "qué" – "qué bien"
  e) "Tener" expressions – "tengo que…" (I've got to…)
  f) Idioms – "lo pasé estupendamente (I had a great time)
  g) If you can use different tenses:

juego	I play
voy a jugar	I'm going to play
jugaré	I will play
jugué	I played
jugaba	I used to play
me gustaría	I would like

HIGHER LEVEL

At this level you will be required to write a letter (formal or informal) in which you will be asked to write about past, present and future events and to express personal opinions. You will also be asked to write a text which demonstrates your ability to write descriptively or imaginatively, for example, an article, account, letter, publicity material.

- Obviously, a lot of what was said for Foundation Tier still applies here. Do make sure you cover all the points and check for mistakes.

- At this level, the examiner will be looking for a good command of tenses, so as well as the present, preterite and immediate future, you must know the future, perfect and imperfect really well.

- The following constructions are worth learning:

estar a punto de	to be on the point of
estar para	to be about to
volver a	to do something again
tardar en	to take so long doing something
mientras + imperfect	while someone was doing something
ojalá (+ subjunctive)	if only
lo (+ adjective):	
lo importante	the most important thing

WRITING TIPS

- Bring in some of the following for which you will be given credit:

primero	first	aunque	although
en primer lugar	firstly	apenas	hardly, scarcely
para empezar	to start with	en lugar de	instead of
por fin	finally	además de	as well as
finalmente	eventually	a pesar de	in spite of
por una parte	on the one hand	a causa de	because of
por otra parte	on the other hand	en cuanto a	with regard to
por lo visto	evidently	tal vez, acaso	perhaps
según parece	apparently	a lo mejor	probably, maybe
de todas formas	anyway	sin duda	no doubt
en efecto	indeed	o sea	that is to say
en realidad	in fact	así que	anyway
según	according to		

- The following impersonal verbs are useful:

interesar (me interesa)	to be interested in (I am interested in)
me interesaría	I would be interested in
encantar (me encanta)	to love (I love)
entusiasmar (me entusiasma)	to be keen on (I am keen on)
apetecer (me apetece)	to fancy (I fancy)
hacer falta (me hace falta)	to need (I need)
gustar (me gusta)	to like (I like)

- At this level you need to expand as much as possible, so join sentences together with words like "que" "cuando" "donde" "porque". A good way to expand your work is to ask yourself a series of questions: what? when? why? where? how? etc.

- Try to bring in opinions:

en mi opinión	in my opinion
me parece que	I think that
quisiera	I should like
espero que	I hope that
estar a favor de	to be in favour of
estar en contra de	to be against
me opongo totalmente a	I'm totally opposed to
me pregunto si	I wonder if
me sorprende que	I'm surprised that
(no) estoy de acuerdo	I (don't) agree
yo creo que	I think that
lo siento mucho pero	I'm very sorry but
me hace mucha ilusión	I'm looking forward to
tu carta me hizo mucha ilusión	I was thrilled to get your letter
¿qué opinas de…?	what's your opinion of…?

Answers

◆ Ejercicio (School Subjects)
page 25

1. ciencias	2. dibujo	3. inglés	4. cocina
5. historia	7. música	6. alemán	8. religión

◆ Sopa de letras (Jobs)
page 32

```
J  M  M  E  R  O  C  A  M  R  A  M
M  E  D  I  T  O  N  G  E  C  E  A
O  D  F  O  C  A  M  E  D  D  O  R
A  C  L  A  G  R  Y  N  I  C  A  I
P  I  U  E  M  E  H  C  I  A  C  N
P  A  N  R  R  I  O  N  H  M  T  E
A  T  E  M  A  N  C  R  O  A  R  R
E  C  R  E  C  E  A  A  S  R  E  O
C  A  T  O  T  G  M  M  J  E  F  E
I  N  S  R  O  N  A  A  T  R  O  S
C  U  A  R  I  R  C  P  A  H  C
S  A  S  M  A  R  E  T  R  A  C  A
```

◆ Crucigrama: en el hotel
page 59

1. piscina	2. individual	3. ducha	4. jabón
5. desayuno	6. ascensor	7. recepcionista	8. comedor
9. pensión	10. persona	11. llave	

◆ Rompecabezas (Clothes and Jewellery)
page 86

plátano es (it's a banana)

◆ Sopa de letras (Clothes)
page 87

```
S  A  G  I  N  O  L  A  C  N  A  A
O  C  Z  C  A  M  F  R  O  C  T  P
S  A  A  A  H  A  O  L  B  E  A  A
O  M  P  M  L  A  A  L  U  N  B  B
R  O  A  D  I  T  U  Q  O  O  V  R
E  G  A  E  N  S  A  R  T  E  E  I
U  I  C  A  H  E  A  S  O  S  J
Q  R  P  S  C  R  S  T  R  E  J
A  B  N  I  B  D  I  A  A  R  O  C
V  A  T  M  L  D  P  E  S  R  E  J
Q  O  O  A  O  A  Y  E  S  R  E  J
B  S  F  C  Z  A  T  A  B  R  O  C
```

◆ Rompecabezas (Transport)
page 95

1. taxi	2. barco	3. autobús	4. avión
5. moto	6. bicicleta	7. pie	8. tren

Acknowledgements

The author and publisher would like to acknowledge the following for the use of copyright material:
ABC; Banco de Bilbao; Consorcio regional de transportes de Madrid; El Corte Inglés; El Olivio Bar; Glaxo; *¡Hola!*; Oficina de información y turismo Pamplona; Pizza-Pizza; Ya.

Every effort has been made to trace copyright holders but the publisher will be pleased to make the necessary arrangements at the first opportunity if there are any omissions.

The author and publisher would like to thank the following for their assistance:
Janine Drake for editing the materials; Marisa Julián for the Native Speaker check.